THE CHESS PLAYS

FISH...MEN
and
KING WITHOUT A CASTLE

TWO PLAYS

BY

Cándido Tirado

NoPassport Press

The Chess Plays
Fish Men and King Without a Castle
by Cándido Tirado
Volume copyright 2021.

Playwright's Notes
Foreword by Jason Ramirez
Invocation by Migdalia Cruz
Director's Notes: *Fish...Men* by Edward Torres
The Theatre of Fantastic Realism by Carmen Rivera
Director's Notes: *King Without A Castle* by Michael John Garces

All Rights Reserved.

For performance rights, contact:
A3 Artists Agency
Ron Gwiazda -- 646-486-4600
ron.gwiazda@a3artistsagency.com
350 Fifth Avenue - 38th floor
NYC, NY 10118

NoPassport Press
PO Box 1786
South Gate, CA 90280 USA
Nopassport.org

ISBN: 978-1-387-11649-2

DEDICATION

To Carmen Rivera, for your unconditional love, support, and for teaching me about the world, while challenging me to become a complete person. To my mentor, Guillermo Gentile, for sharing his theatrical discoveries and knowledge, and entrusting me with his theory. To my abuelo, Tómas Tirado, for gifting me the love of story. To my mother, Basilia "Bacha" Meléndez, for believing in intelligence "something no one can take away." To my sister Maria Tirado for your generosity of spirit. I couldn't imagine my life without you.

A BIG Thank You to Latino Theater, for opening your spaces to me, and without whom I wouldn't be the playwright that I am today. Puerto Rican Traveling Theatre, Repertorio Español, INTAR, Teatro Vista. Urban Theater, Pregones, Latino Experimental Fantastic Theater, Shaman Theater, Hero Theatre, Afro Caribbean Theatre, The Family Theater, Pregones, Nuyorican Poets Café, Nosotros Teatro, Marietta's New Theater in the Square, El Ateneo Puertorriqueño, The Guadalupe Arts Center, Bregamos Community Theater, and to Independent Producers: Ralph Mercado, David Maldonado, David Rodriguez, Henry Cárdenas, Mickey Oquendo and Elizardi Castro.

SPECIAL THANKS

To my "spiritual sister" Migdalia Cruz. Caridad Svich and No Passport for the publication of these two plays. Miriam Colón, Max Ferra, Gilberto Zaldívar, Rene Bush, Robert Federico, Ilka Tanya Payan, Gloria Zelaya, Juan Shamsul Alam, Maria Estevez, Edward Torres, Sandra Marquez, Ivan Vega, Miranda Gonzalez, Elisa Bocanegra, Lou Moreno, Michael John Garces, Jason Ramirez, Roberto Ramos Perea, Elisha Miranda, Nikole Abrego, Ngina Williams, Paula Raflo, Elisa Loti Stein, Tanya Palmer, Kristin Leahey, and my close friends and my most ardent supporters Edward Torres, Jerald Times, Michael Camacho and Ylon Schwartz.

PLAYWRIGHT'S NOTES

When I graduated from Lehman College, I decided to do two things with my life, "Write Plays" and "Play Chess." Today, after 40 years in the "milonga," as my mentor Guillermo Gentile used to say, I can affirm unequivocally I have achieved what I set out to do. From the moment chess was introduced into my life, it spoke to me. After playing millions of games, I can still remember my very first game, which I lost, but should have won. I still haven't gotten over that defeat. While in college, I studied the game and played in my first few tournaments. After graduating, I won some individual tournaments and was part of a team that won an East Coast Championship. I've defeated a Grandmaster (highest rank a chess player can achieve) and some International Masters (second-highest rank) in tournament play. I also defeated players who went on to become grandmasters.

In the 1980s through 1990s, Washington Square Park was a mecca for chess players, and I was a fixture there when taking a break from writing. I was an extra in the movie Searching for Bobby Fischer, and I even got a close-up. Later, I became an assistant coach for a middle school chess team that won multiple championships, including National, State, and City titles, under the helm of my longtime friend, chess senior-master, and poet, Jerald Times. I was also a chess commentator in the 1984 world championship match. I attained the title of National Chess Master, which ranks me in the top 1% of the country. One of my proudest moments as a chess player occurred when former World Champion Boris Spassky sat across from me at the legendary Manhattan Chess Club, and I refuted a chess move he played.

Why this walk down the memory chess lane? Simple answer: I wished to merge my love for these two great art forms. The Chess Plays is the result of that wish. *King Without a Castle* was first developed at the INTAR Playwriting Lab led by Maria Irene Fornes. At that same time, I attended workshops in The Theatre of Fantastic Realism with Guillermo Gentile. These two great workshops fused together to give *King Without a Castle life*. Later, *King Without a Castle* was selected to participate in the Sundance Playwright's Lab. It also won a New York Foundation for The Arts Fellowship. Moreover, it received a workshop production at Castillo Theater, directed by Guillermo Gentile. *King Without a Castle* received its Off-Broadway premiere at the Puerto Rican Traveling Theatre, directed by Michael John Garces.

About the time *King Without a Castle* was receiving its Off-Broadway production, I had developed a friendship with the talented New York—Puerto Rican playwright and theoretician Tee Saralegui. One day, as we discussed dramatic theory, we walked into Washington Square Park's chess tables and the idea for *Fish...Men* came to me. The first draft of *Fish...Men* received a fellowship from New York Foundation for the Arts. However, I wasn't satisfied with the final product. Later, I came to the realization I could use the world of chess hustlers as a metaphor for genocide, a crime humanity happily commits over and over again. I started researching genocides that have occurred throughout the history of the world. Needless to say, this was depressing as hell. But as the stories for these characters began to fall into place, the play started to evolve. *Fish…Men* received its world premiere at The Goodman Theatre in collaboration with Teatro Vista, directed by Edward Torres. The production received four Jeff nominations and an Edgerton Foundation New Play Award (TCG). It was also nominated for a Steinberg/ATCA New Play Award. Later, it received its New York premiere at INTAR, directed by Lou Moreno.

Both Plays were extremely challenging to write. With *King Without a Castle*, the reason was its theoretical nature. I had to strictly adhere to The Theater of Fantastic Realism theory, which I was learning at the time. I couldn't deviate into Realism, Naturalism, or Absurd theater. (See Carmen Rivera's essay in this book on The Theatre of Fantastic Realism.) *Fish…Men* was challenging because of its structure. The play is written in "Real-Time." A "Real-Time" play unfolds in front of the audience. The duration of the performance parallels that of the Play's action.

Not only have I been able to achieve my goals to "Write Plays" and "Play Chess," but this publication also allows me to share my love for these two great art forms with you.

                                           Cándido Tirado
                                              July 25, 2021

Foreword – **Cándido Tirado's The Chess Plays**

For years, the Nuyorican Theatre Movement, which commenced with the groundbreaking work of Pedro Pietri, Miguel Piñero, and other pioneers of the Nuyorican Poet's Café, has continued to thrive with iconic productions created by theatrical companies including the Puerto Rican Traveling Theatre, INTAR Theatre, Latino Experimental Fantastic Theatre, and of course, the world famous Repertorio Español. Though dozens of prolific Latinx writers have had plays produced by these collectives, one would be hard-pressed to identify a playwright who has been as widely produced, and critically acclaimed over decades, as master playwright, **Cándido Tirado**. Tirado's theatrical oeuvre and professional mentorship of playwrights and artists has secured decades-long praise from academics including Alberto Sandoval-Sanchez and John Antush, distinguished playwrights Caridad Svich and Migdalia Cruz, producers Robert Federico and Miriam Colón, Pulitzer Prize winner Stephen Adly Guirgis, and crossover artists including Modesto Lacen and entertainment icon, Curtis "50 Cent" Jackson. Tirado's unique abilities, in all theatrical vocations, including playwriting, directing, producing, and teaching have earned Tirado a reputation as a no-nonsense, theatrical powerhouse. This two-play collection allows the reader to experience Tirado's ever-evolving process while highlighting works separated by two decades of politically-charged art.

To understand the work of Cándido Tirado is to delve into the theatrical theories of Argentinian playwright and artist, Guillermo Gentile, and his theoretical framework, the Theater of Fantastic Realism. In Gentile's own assessment, "The Theater of Fantastic Realism, [is] a revolutionary kind of theater that often uses metaphor and the irrational to explore the innermost desires and dreams of the characters...the Theater of Fantastic Realism, or Theatre for a New Mythology, is a metaphorical theatre, where the interpretations are multiple and different. It doesn't communicate with the audience as a whole, but with each one of the spectators, giving to each one a personal and unique experience." One cannot help but see the connection between the characters in *King Without a Castle* (1983) without feeling the connection in Gentile's own pursuit of the fantastic. The play begins with Tirado launching his audience deep into Gentile's "irrational" framework:

TIME
The past, present, and future happening simultaneously.

PLACE
Anywhere that people are ruled by the past but are struggling to change the present for a better future.

The world inhabited by Danny, Isabel, and Soledad mirrors that of the irrational world of the fantastic. Characters' worldly obsessions defy the constraints of time and space, as they re-visit each other through a continuum broken by the rigors of the natural world. As experienced in an exploration of the "irrational"

A-Theory, introduced by physicist Richard Gale and following the theoretical underpinnings of metaphysician L.M.E. McTaggart's canonical treatise *"The Unreality of Time,"* the juxtaposition of time which envelops this family's epic "chess fantasia" seeks remedy in Gentile's "new mythology." How else would it be possible for Danny to exist in the same metaphysical world as his own father or for Isabel to remain 25 years old her entire life? Thus, through an exploration of McTaggart's proposed unreality, or what I would reconstitute as Gentile/Tirado's "irrationality" of time, the A-Theory experience allows the audience a series of positions which run from either "the far past, through the near past, and into the present," or as in the case of Tirado's masterwork *Fish...Men* (2000), a trajectory which allows an exploration of the present, through the near future, to the far future.

"The ellipses in *Fish...Men* is a way to show that men come from fish. The creatures that later on went to be land creatures, and later human beings, had their origins in the sea. **The ellipsis is a marker of time**. It took millions of years for that to happen." As was the case with the absurdist playwrights of the twentieth-century who also utilized McTaggart's through-line of time to develop dramas where characters, and their dramatic arcs, could co-exist in the same theatrical space, Tirado's characters are both trapped and freed by the explorations of worlds which cannot be centered in the rational mind, or in continuous, unadulterated time. Here, chess tables serve as sacred spaces which defy time in juxtaposition to the discussed

10

carving of dead presidents into the Black Hills, the destruction of Mayan culture, or the myriad of injustices borne of the Holocaust. A vast array of meta-theatrical criticisms are made throughout the play by the chess-playing, social critics characterized within the play itself.

King Without a Castle succeeds in destroying Aristotle's unities of time, place, and action (though truly developed by the neo-classicists) while heralding the absurd techniques of scribes who began to be produced in simultaneity with Gentile's fantastic theatrical theories (1950s – 1970s). The influence of these masters, many of which fueled the origins of the Latin American theatrical boom of the second half of the twentieth-century, weigh heavily on the theoretical/theatrical work of Gentile, and later, Tirado. As Tirado explains, "…the absurdist was my first love. Beckett, Adamov, Ionesco. Read Artaud. The use of symbols and metaphors in their plays really informed me. And it helped me recognize those absurd moments in our lives that are hard to explain. However, I had a fantastical mind already, even before meeting Guillermo Gentile. He gave me a vessel, a way of thinking about a play that had embedded a technique of approaching the work. It was an easy transference for me. The way I looked at the world, and Guillermo's theory, was comparable. An easy fit." To experience a play written by Tirado, whether early works including *Some People Have All the Luck* (1980) or more recent plays including *Momma's Boyz* (1999) or *La Canción* (2016), is to journey into a Lewis Carroll-esque kaleidoscope where the rabbit hole becomes the normative world of the play. We, as audience, take the trip through time and space and cast off the "mortal coils" which preoccupy most conventional theatre produced since the el movimiento del teatro vanguardia of the 1970s.

The trajectory of Tirado's work and his innate ability to carry theoretical threads of the Fantastic Theatre throughout his canon, allow for varied texts which include historical biographies, musicals, hip hop fables, and Latinx reconstructions (as seen in his brilliant, unproduced *Palladium*)[1]. Simultaneously, Tirado's productions serve as a parranda steeped in the theoretical underpinnings of Victor Turner's promised [Latinx] communitas while avoiding the often-simplistic nature of post-modern pastiche and commercial performative practice. In this way, I believe that Tirado absorbs Gentile's fantastic as well as the aesthetics of the absurd, and creates a new, hybrid form of dramaturgical practice which utilizes the independentista decl(ar/am)ations of Pedro Albizu-Campos and Lolita Lebron. Tirado himself, throughout his decades of artistic production, has become a "king in search of a theatrical castle." As the Native American Jerome warns John in *Fish...Men* "You're not taking my table the way they stole my land...I don't want people to forget that this continent was and will always be Indigenous land."

The comparisons between *King Without a Castle*, and iconic Nuyorican provocateur Pedro Pietri's

---

[1] Co-written with Carmen Rivera and David Maldonado, 2006.

masterpiece, *The Masses are Asses* (1974) truly enlighten us to the genius of Tirado's ability to adapt commercial theatrical productions (take *Fish...Men* or Tirado and Carmen Rivera's biographical *Celia: The Life and Music of Celia Cruz* (2007) into an irrational fantastic epoch which easily travels through time and space. Tirado's praise of past Latinx playwriting masters, and their impact on his own socio-political ideologies is noted in his reflection that "Pedro Pietri's plays should be mentioned with the absurd writers. He was up there with them even if not recognized. Although I like the absurd writers, they were white men of a certain time which informed them of how far down humanity can fall and all the pretenses fall alongside with it. After all, they saw their world collapse during WWII." This negation of the colonizing factors often involved in mentorship of playwrights (and for that matter, politicians and scholars) is demonstrated throughout Tirado's work. I, for one, recall a production of *XY Stories* (2002), where a character who is written to represent Tirado himself received nightly applause when he exclaimed "Henry Kissinger is a war criminal."

As was the case with Pietri and Piñero, warnings against the colonizing factors which hinder Latinx public discourse thread the work of Tirado. This centuries-long colonial practice of institutional poverty by the U.S. government serves as an indictment of what Tirado calls "lumping" and is best demonstrated in the

---

[2] Co-written within a collective of eight Latinx playwrights with Tirado serving as dramaturg.

vociferous opinions of Jerome in *Fish...Men*. Tirado has mastered a sharp theatrical critique of post-Vietnam, neo-colonial indoctrination as well as a denunciation of the tamer, yet just as destructive, limitations of post-millennial neo-liberalism. **I argue that Tirado was "woke" before most of us set our alarm clocks and we are now attempting to catch up.** Tirado's brilliant deconstruction of "lumping" argues "when the white American tries to combine all those people who come from different countries into one group, hence, creating the new identity...lumping [becomes] a clean and effective way where the Anglos can put us in a nicely packaged box." Tirado's decades-long advice for Latinx writers to self-produce work, in lieu of accepting economic funds from mainstream producers, is more important in our post-pandemic world than ever before. In doing so, we seize the monetary modes of production and minority artists can avoid being "lumped" in with groups who may write from differing histories, sociologies, and languages. The commercial theatre's agreed upon, yet unethical practice of lumping disguised as neo-liberal pan-Latinidad, makes Tirado's success all the more worthy of praise. His accolades reach within the television and film industry, multi-cultural student groups at institutions as varied as the economically privileged New School, and all-inclusive, open enrollment student bodies working with him at Baruch College of the City University of New York.

Fish...Men's opening stage direction: "In the darkness, the loud ticking of a clock is heard" heralds Jerome's ongoing discussion of geo-political matters, post-colonialism, mass genocide and the fantastical realistic chessboard which serves as the representative "theatre of war" simulacrum which resonates in the work of Pietri, Gentile, and Tirado. This clock represents both the world of the chess match as well as the Doomsday Clock which is currently sitting at ten seconds from midnight, following the "irrational" presidency of a man who entered the political sphere by stating that Mexicans were "rapists and murderers," and constituencies including Latinx Long Island citizens, African-American Baltimore residents, and U.S. bound immigrants from "shithole countries" who "live like animals." The chess clock serves as Jerome's warning regarding the end of the world: "If you just shut your mouths for once and listen, you will hear mankind's clock winding down, signaling mankind's inevitable and most deserving end. And once the time on the clock runs out, it cannot be rewound. Tick... Tock... Tick... Tock."

Further, Tirado's audience is made to experience an exploration of world conflict through the multi-national characters in *Fish...Men* as they adeptly maneuver the geo-political strata through the international game of chess.

> **JEROME**: Let me put it this way. Imagine this: two countries in the middle of a brutal, unnecessary war, call it a draw and start negotiating from anew? What do you think, Cash? Think about it. Two countries about to nuke each other into oblivion agree to a draw, shake hands, pack up, and go home. The

concept of a draw is genius. The draw can save humanity!

Yet, within this unattainable goal, Tirado reminds us of the players who control the game, as we are reminded, "The golden rule...hustlers don't hustle hustlers." This brilliant line reflects Tirado's lifelong mastery of the game of chess and the "game of life" and reminds me of the equally brilliant theatrical imagination of Suzan-Lori Parks. In her Pulitzer Prize winning play *Topdog/Underdog* (2000), the character of Lincoln (a black man impersonating the real Abraham Lincoln in a penny arcade) warns against the dangers of centuries-long colonization and continued cultural gameplay ensconced within the unwinnable 3 Card Monte hustle:

> **LINCOLN**: Its like thuh cards. And ooooh you certainly was persistent. But you was in such a hurry to learn thuh last move that you didn't bother learning thuh first one. That was yr mistake. Cause its the first move that separates the Player from the Played. And thuh first move is to know that there aint no winning. Taadaaa! It may look like you got a chance but the only time you pick right is **when thuh man lets you**...Thought you was uh Player. But I played you, bro.

The similarity between these two pre-9/11 masterpieces serves as a warning against theatrical games of war, controlled and perpetuated on a global scale by those who have always held, and continue to hold, our lives in their blood-soaked hands. Explorations of poverty, privilege, discrimination, and in the case of *Fish...Men*, the remembrance of two separate holocausts in Europe and Guatemala (as a stand-in for the hundreds of thousands of lives lost in 20th and 21st century Latin America) are dramatically (re)played on these "game" boards, Tirado's chess squares and Parks' folding card(board) table remind me of the classic cult favorite, *War Games* (1983), released in the same year as *King Without a Castle*. In this John Badham film, the apocalyptic children's video game entitled "Global Thermonuclear War," and the military industrial complex's titular offer, "Shall we play a game?" is eventually reconciled by the computer program Joshua, who determines that these types of genocidal human desires can only be eliminated when we all conclude that "the only way to win...is not to play."

How can we not identify with the ancient rites of gameplaying, as in the case of chess, card games of skill, video games, and the strategic options which lay bare the irrational destruction of humanity in governmental "theatres" of war? All these "games" lay bare our necessity to reinvent centuries-old stories through our embedded cultural mythologies. As Danny explains, "There isn't a future for chess players who think they know everything. They're roaches. That's why they can't be champions. I bust my ass searching for the truth in these sixty-four squares. I'll do it. I'll make it. You'll see. I'm the best. The best! I swear it to you. I'm going to make it." Unfortunately, as Soledad reminds us is the eventual endgame in the world of Tirado's Chess Plays, "That's a dream! A dream! Live in reality!"

In discussing his play, *With Folded Wings*, Guillermo Gentile notes that his dramatic work "…tries to rescue the eternal values of what is legendary, magical, and mythological. The early stories were learned sitting on the laps of our grandparents and harmonized us with a world of values we could not understand. Our first lessons were through a fantastic understanding of reality; beyond any logic." In this way, the illogical step of "killing one's father" has served as theatrical quest for 2500 years of dramatic production. The examples provided by Oedipus' crossroads encounter with Laius, Hamlet's staged mousetrap of Claudius, or Biff's kitchen table destruction of Willy Loman's irrational dreamscape, are "given light" in Joseph Campbell's seminal text, *The Hero With a Thousand Faces*, as we are forced to (ir)rationalize Step Nine of the famed *"Hero's Journey"* – namely, "Atonement with the Father." This atonement provides Tirado an opportunity to explore the problematic relationships between Latino men and their fathers while providing a foundation for both *King Without a Castle* and *Fish…Men*.

Soledad posits this socio-cultural concern in *King Without a Castle* while arguing, "You're always imagining you're playing against your father. That's freaky (realizes she said something she shouldn't have said). I'm sorry. I shouldn't have said that." The contentious relationship between fathers and sons, described by Campbell as a

18

"war within the shadows," serves to help us understand the Theatre of Fantastic Realism's explorations of human relations within a mythological framework, as well as in the contentious worlds created within Tirado's own dramatic canon. Gentile reminds us that "The ancient battle between the forces of light and darkness (shadows), between angels and demons, beats within each of our hearts, and from that place illuminates our world while determining (creating) our reality." What better mythological trope could be retold within the fantastic and irrational world of *King Without a Castle* than that of the "killing of the father." Further, whether we examine *Fish...Men's* opening sensory illustration of "darkness," or Danny's preoccupation with shadows, Tirado provides a metaphysical connection between ancient mythos, current socio-political events, or the complexities of representative Latinidad within a 21st century, pan-Latinx shadow-play.

> **DANNY:** You don't understand. Our fathers tried to kill us, but they couldn't!
> **SOLEDAD:** My father didn't try to kill me. It was an accident. He crashed his car into the river when a truck ran him off the road.
> **DANNY:** Fathers are killers.
> **SOLEDAD:** You want me to hate my father because you hate yours.
> **DANNY:** He wanted to kill you.
> **SOLEDAD:** He loved me!
> **DANNY:** He's still calling you to the bottom of the river.

Grounded within the structural shadows of *King Without a Castle*, and bound within the theoretical structure of the Theatre of Fantastic Realism, Tirado provides an exploration of patricide (as noted by Joseph Campbell) for the sake of healing.

> **DANNY:** (Jumping around watching his shadow jumping around, too.) They're very playful.
> **SOLEDAD:** You don't understand. Shadows don't like being shadows. They hate being dragged around and being forced to spend their lives leaning against walls. They envy and want to replace their owners.

Tirado's dialogue highlights Danny's obsession with shadows, which in turn, replicates Soledad's own obsession with television commercials, drawing a comparison of obsessive-compulsive disorder to Peter Shaffer's masterpiece on similar themes, *Equus* (1973). Though both characters realize that the only way "to leave our shadows behind" will be to "look at the light," it is only through the tedious obsessive replaying of "mind games" that our intense human flaws demand we philosophize a familial connection to that which is most damaging. The psychological destruction perpetrated on humans by their parents before birth, is the same ancient mythology argued for by Gentile—our own psyche feeds the characters in *King Without a Castle*, and pat[mat]ricide will be our only escape. When Danny remarks "I wasn't lucky to be born. I was born because I was the strongest sperm," Isabel decimates him by replying "You were lucky a horse beat your father for the abortion money." However, what Tirado creates within his Chess Plays is the enlightened promise of the game of life, and what this game offers us in our creation of self. Note how Danny creates his own self-worth within the confines of chess:

> **DANNY:** Because I'm good. I'm going to be the best chess player in the world.
> **ISABEL:** You can't always be who you want to be.
> **DANNY:** Why not? I'll be whoever I want to be. And I'm going to be the greatest chess player that has ever lived.
> **ISABEL:** I always had this wonderful feeling you were going to be something more than a chess player.
> **DANNY:** If I'm not going to be who I want to be, then who am I going to be?
> **ISABEL:** I don't know. I'm just telling you of a marvelous feeling I have. Call it mother's intuition.

The necessity to kill one's father to redeem a part of the world, whether it be modern psychology of religious doctrine, proposes our existence within a time continuum where there can be only one "father" who makes the decisions, eats the food, has the sex, and governs the spoils of history. It is through the ritual of killing the egoic memory of the father that a male child becomes a man - in turn, defeating him at his own game, or as Isabel explains, "There's nothing you can do. It's been going on forever. Fathers always take over their sons." The hustlers gathered in *Fish...Men* know this all too well as they cannibalize each other, both financially, and psychologically, to survive. Though seemingly irrational, the dictates of government, corporate profit and ethics, and yes, the game of chess are all contingent upon this societal patricide. It is only in our acceptance of this murder that we continue to exist, as noted by the two women serving as Danny's mother/lovers.

Further, Tirado utilizes the act of mirroring his characters in much the same way that Pietri does in *The Masses are Asses*, or Reinaldo Povod in *La Puta Vida Trilogy* (1986), paying careful attention to the metatheatrical doubling of Danny Jr. to Danny Sr., Isabel to Soledad, Soledad's parents to Isabel and Danny Sr., hamsters to babies, and strikingly, chess pieces to soldiers. Role doubling, as is the case within much absurdist drama (Genet's work comes to mind immediately) resonates throughout *King Without a Castle*, and later, within the structure of *Fish...Men*. This meta-theatrical device is made transparent as Danny notes "They're not a real family. They're actors" strikingly a resonant chord of similarity with the godfather of Latina/o theatre, José Triana's masterpiece, *La noche de los asesinos* (1957). Of note, Isabel and Soledad provide the necessary solution to the existence of multiple theatrical characters, human beings, or chess pieces existing on the same plane of existence, or chessboard, as they debate:

> **ISABEL:** Here they are! (Hands the box to Soledad.)

SOLEDAD: What are my parents doing in a box? (Soledad takes out two urns from the box.)
ISABEL: They were collecting dust out here, dear.
SOLEDAD: That's so thoughtful of you, Isabel.
ISABEL: How sad!
SOLEDAD: What's sad? What?
ISABEL: It breaks my heart, seeing your parents in different urns. I wouldn't want to spend the rest of eternity separated from Daniel.
SOLEDAD: You're right. Why didn't I think about that? (Soledad pours the ashes of one urn into the other urn.) Now, they'll be together forever.

While *King Without a Castle* expertly utilizes theories embedded in The Theatre of Fantastic Realism, combined with Tirado's intense knowledge of Latinx/Nuyorican absurdist dramatic practices, the staging of *Fish...Men* necessitates the interpretation of a skilled director. The implementation of specific chess strategies embedded in the actor's sense memory as dialogue, allows the audience to share in the aforementioned communitas, or imagined communities proposed by scholars Victor Turner, Benedict Anderson and Juan Flores. Fish Men exists in a post-millennial, yet pre-9/11 Runyon-esque world, known intimately by lifelong New Yorker, Cándido Tirado. Racing forms, street hustles, and various ethnicities all living in NYC promotes *Fish...Men* as a Ground Zero reconstruction of our own visual/aural experience filled with an overbearing sense of that day's loss, and reminiscent of Ninety-Two's own nightmare of being chased by "tall chimneys." This theoretical exploration of the play can be further illuminated by Jerome who recalls "When you're up high in a tall skyscraper, and you look down, people become dots. Dots! The Great Spirit looks at us vertically. To Him, there's no difference between one dot and another. The problem with human beings is that we live in a horizontal plane. When we look at one another, all we see is our differences."

Fish...Men is a critique on the economic wasteland of NYC, co-existing with Wall Street's decadence, in the days preceding 9/11. Ninety Two's refusal to continue to service bankers and brokers is tied to his refusal to remain witness to its economic atrocities upon the disadvantaged of the world, and for that matter, the horrors he witnessed during the Holocaust. Tirado explains the complexities of living as a politically-active artist during this complex time in our history, and specifically, as a native New York resident, prior to and since, September 11, 2001:

I believe that in 1998 there was a chess championship match played on the observation deck of one of the World Trade Center buildings. I went to watch the match several times. The original *Fish...Men* mentioned that match, but when the Trade Center collapsed, I decided to remove the reference. **My play deals with man's inhumanity towards man in its totality, and I didn't want to get bogged down with national politics.** One of the critics who didn't like the play questioned why it didn't talk about the WTC. As it was not a

genocide, I couldn't put it in my
play. Besides, the hustlers' way of life after the towers came down didn't change much. Chess players are good at compartmentalizing. Perhaps business went down a little
bit. However, the towers coming down affected me differently, and that was adapted into the play. When the first plane hit, I was walking across the street from the tower. When I started working on the play, the sentiment was very negative. The point I was making was about how horrible humanity really is. However, after the towers came down, I remember September 12 and how spiritual that day was—how New Yorkers began to help one another—when the firemen asked for food in less than an hour, they had too much food—when they asked for socks, in no time, they received more than they needed. That gave me a hint of how, after a tragedy, the human spirit always shines through. That's when the tone of my play changed. I wrote the first draft of *Fish...Men* in 1998, but I believe the final draft, or at least a draft I was happy with, wasn't written until about 2010.

Fish...Men, as is the case with most great plays, captures its time without the necessity of referring to specific events from our recollective conscience. It lives across time as exemplified by the dictates of the Theatre of Fantastic Realism. This is as much a 9/11 play as it is an apocalyptic revelation of the intricacies of God/Man/Spirit – a Shamanistic healing ritual which serves as a testimonio for the atrocities of our shared 20th century holocausts in Europe/Guatemala/Rwanda and elsewhere, resolved within the confines of a theatrical chess match. Further, Tirado provides a re-envisioning of the Four Horsemen through dual Revelations of John, that imagined in the last book of the Bible as well as the truncated explications of our Belarusian chess player. *Fish...Men's* 9/11 revelations mirror New Testament parables with fish falling from a dark sky, with John explaining "Is not who see him first but who dinner plate he land in" as a horrific reminder of the "falling" persons captured in stills of the destruction of the Twin Towers.

The symbolism of Rey drinking water from a park fountain positions him as a modern "king of kings" or literally, **Rey Reyes**, the deliverer of fish who Jerome envisions as having "the same look my father had before he walked into the desert..." However, Washington Square Park, a mere mile from the actual Ground Zero, is where these fish are collected for consumption, or as Jerome notes "...a coral reef for chess players. Chess brings us all together for better or worse." Tirado's own explanation that he "stumbled onto the Mayan story of the *Fish...Men*...[and] the crude idea that hustlers call their marks fish" substantiates Cash's history lesson on genocide, warning "I don't swim at the beach. It's like swimming in a watery cemetery of my ancestors." John's "pony" picks are considered to be in search of salvation and through the direct intersession of Rey's sacrificial playing and Ninety-Two's prophecies of doom, may be eventually saved from eternal damnation. After all, it is Ninety-Two's philosophy on fish, "You throw a fish line and hope they grab it and hold on for dear life," which mirrors his own ideology. The characters,

John specifically with his "pony" picks, are all looking for souls to save, as Ninety-Two has attempted decades earlier with his sister and Rey in his redemption of his own chess-hustled savior, Bernie. Rey and Ninety-Two are in the business of saving souls, a running theme in the work of Damon Runyon, and the park serves as their own "Save-a Soul Mission." The symbolic name-play becomes clearer throughout the play, with John Zhuk as the linguistically simple, itinerant gambler of yore (Juan Bobo), Jerome Guerrero (Warmaker) as the Comanche warrior, Adam Kirchbaum (first man) as the progenitor of the game, and Godfrey Cash as the literal "God of money." However, Tirado is adamant in his belief that "community matters more than corporate greed" reminding me that the final moments of Fish Men allows the audience to experience "the hustlers stop their hustling to watch Adam play a friendly game of chess." A human moment of reflection shared by character and audience alike.

Moreover, John's monolingual explanation that there is only "One language in world. Chess!" contradicts Cash's multilingual style of play (economic survival), providing a comparison to the Old Testament parable of the Tower of Babel -- multiple voices unable to comprehend each other. In the world of *Fish...Men*, chess is the only universal language which can be understood by all humanity. However, Rey as the "redeemer" is meant to establish a [New] world order when he warns "According to the *Popol Vuh*, these Fish Men, half men - half fish, came down to earth from the sky to destroy the wicked, those who preyed on the weak and those who dealt in the misery of others. I'm a Fish Man. I came down to set the park straight. You guys took advantage of Bernie. And anybody that fucks with Bernie has to deal with me. He can't defend himself. But, that's what I'm here for. Payback time!"

Tirado's Chess Plays are an exploration of what makes humanity survive. The individual choices we make and the sacrifices and hustles which dominate our lives. Our limitations and flaws are exorcised as we watch the performance of Tirado's characters, who are more than willing to provide critique of the strategies we enact on a daily basis -- in our histories and ideologies, and for that matter, the "irrational" games we manipulate to survive the harsh realities of the world. Tirado's criticism of institutions is symbolized through the playing of the game. While the Guatemalan Massacre creates a sense of paranoia for Rey and Bernie, Jerome exhibits his own through his protestations against the U.S. government's theft of native land, and the seemingly simple realization that John and Cash are simultaneously attempting to steal his table. The Chess Plays delve into our past and how we remain traumatized by it in our present state of being. Isabel's frozen state which keeps her bound to her twenty-fifth year is a coping mechanism. Otherwise, how could she continue to survive in the harsh environment and social status of being Latina in a brutal, patriarchal society that considers mass genocide a solution to world affairs. Again, as Gentile has posited, the performative nature of the irrational world makes our observation of everyday life possible.

Cash's opinion on Jerome and Ninety-Two's pasts make perfect sense in an irrational world: "Look, our system is predicated on hustling. The strong hustle the weak. The smart hustle the dumb. The informed hustle the uninformed. And on and on. I didn't make the rules, but I abide by them. I'm so proud of both of you. You hustled the system. We're not that different." This difficult realization of ourselves is the sociological work that master playwright Cándido Tirado has illuminated for more than four decades. The Chess Plays are both a philosophical tour de force and a theatrical experience for audience and reader alike. We are left numb at the inexplicable nature of humanity yet hopeful of the possibilities still to come. As resolved by Jerome, "We're all fish trying to avoid the fishing hooks. Some of us are luckier than others."

Punto...

Jason Ramírez, Ph.D.
Professor of Theatre and Humanities
Suffolk County Community College (SUNY)
January 15, 2021

The Basic Principles of Opening An Artist: An Invocation for Cándido Tirado's Life-Work

Moving the Rook to control the center:
After Inauguration 2021, as I sighed with political relief, I thought about Marcel Duchamp. Just like we of the non-upper class, non-white majority clamored for change and equity and a voice in our destiny, Duchamp's Dadaist theories about art engaged his chess master's strategy to confront the assumptions of conventional society by making art with everyday objects of everyday people. His artistic vision terrified the upper classes as he turned a urinal into a piece of ceramic art. People never looked at a urinal the same way again. Is that what makes it Art? Unsurprisingly, both Duchamp and Cándido Tirado joined their chess strategies to their artistic practice. I wonder if idiosyncratic artists like Cándido—who happen to come from humble beginnings—could be whom Duchamp hoped to inspire? What does it mean to be an artist in the 21st Century? "To control the center" and start the game of a "Play?" These two artists give us permission to undo the status quo, create a unique relationship between artist and audience, expanding the field of theater by focusing our gaze and opening our minds to work once subjugated by the majority. They enable an exquisite game of theatrical chess.

King safety & castling:
Men are so fragile. The Queen is always stronger and the players move around her, even though it is the king we need to protect. Don't leave him in

the middle of the board. You need to castle him, so the Queen can do the killing. But that was last year's nightmare. This year the king can be stronger because the Queen protects the king and the king protects her. Equals. Isn't that what we are fighting for? I never had a brother, until I met Cándido Tirado. We were people from a small island who then moved to the mainland borough of the Bronx. The power of finding an artistic sibling opened my world to all the vibrant and inspiring Puerto Rican, Nuyorican and Rican+ others, who all found their feet buried in the Caribbean sand no matter where in the world they found themselves standing. This was life-as-a-writer affirming. A found family.

Development:
Cándido's courage and aggressive word-play taught me how to protect our words by attacking the status quo with logic and relentless debate. His work teaches us how to position our pieces and settle in for the long game—how pragmatic characters with purpose and strategic storylines teach us to play a stronger artistic game.

Freedom:
When we measure the freedom of movement for every piece in chess, we uncover all the possibilities for our pieces to move, thereby developing a winning strategy. When we write our stories with the strength of purpose our ancestors willed to us, we are free to move through our work rooted in history while infusing our ancestral survival spirit into the art. The work of Cándido Tirado exemplifies this freedom in movement through his grounded present resonating with the past to create

original theatrical "checkmates" that make it impossible to ignore his message. You cannot escape the truth. Especially if you're a king.

May those ancestral sea-winds speed us on this journey of shared humanity and history by revealing the words that define our artistic world. *Asè*.

Migdalia Cruz
January 25, 2021

Fish...Men – Director's Note
Esteemed Colleague, Artist and Brother from another Mother.

Fish...Men, impacted me profoundly the first time I read it. When I think of Latino or Latin-X playwrights, Cándido Tirado is a name to be reckoned with. An original New Nuyorican playwright. His other works such as *Momma's Boyz, King Without Castle,* and *First Class* are considered classics within the Latinx play Canon. *Fish... Men,* a play about redemption, addiction, and the spirit of survival has now joined that Canon. Cándido Tirado has chosen to tell us a story about how humanity treats itself. His words are straight, honest and hard-hitting.

The international high stakes game of Chess appears in varied tournaments throughout the world, whether in a park where money and reputation are at stake or at a McDonald's or Starbucks where the bragging rights are always up for grabs. The game is iconic, fluid and at times cut throat.

The world of the intellect, tact and strategy is the setting in Washington Square Park, NYC., where the hustle is alive, vibrant and unforgiving. You can see, hear and feel the rhythm of Chess as the participants vie for respect, and the opportunity to make a living. The action is so alive, that you can hear the clock being smacked, the chess pieces being slammed against the granite table, and the banter of the players all in sync with one another.

Speed is of the essence and out maneuvering your opponent with both mental dexterity and a verbal assault can make a difference between winning and losing. Tirado captures this both in the story telling as well as in the game within the play.

The thought of having to contemplate and ponder your opponent's next move while making yours in order to achieve the ultimate goal of winning before your time runs out on the clock is unbelievable! You must be quick, precise and unrelenting in your strategy.

Tirado draws his characters from real life experience; a recently arrived Russian, a Native American, a Guatemalan and a Holocaust survivor just to name a few. Each character has a personal story of adversity in which they offer up their point of view as immigrants or people of color on the American experience in the United States. Often, this is far from perfect and tragic. Secrets are revealed, humanity is explored, and motives exposed.

I remember going with Tirado to Washington Square Park to see the Chess tables and the gray wall that they stood against. Or the Chess Forum club where Cándido often played on West Fourth St., with his unruly band of characters who were often quick witted and funny. I even witnessed Tirado, a National Master himself, play with ease and tenacity as he made his way through the table in seconds and wiped out his opponent. Impressive to say the least. I knew then that I was a part of something special.

Fish…Men, is filled not with just action but with heart and hope.

Edward Torres
DIRECTOR
January 20, 2021

ABOUT CHESS

One doesn't need to understand chess to understand Fish...Men. There's a basic tutorial on how to read the chess notations at the end of the play. You can find in-depth tutorials on the Internet under "chess notation" with diagrams. If you would like to get some understanding of the game of chess, you can search on YouTube, where there are many free beginner chess videos. You can also join Chess.Com, where you can find lessons to improve your chess, and play players from around the world.

Ten complete chess games have been provided. Each game is given a name. In addition, four short incomplete games have also been provided. Some chess moves are interspersed within the dialogue, and those moves correspond to the dialogue in some manner.

FISH...MEN

A PLAY

CHARACTERS:

REY REYES: (GUATEMALAN) Late Twenties – Early Thirties. Short. Slight built. Looks as if he couldn't hurt a fly. He works as a Computer Programmer. Wears a suit. If you see him walking down the street, you'd think he was a successful young man, but he suffers from undiagnosed PTSD.

ADAM KIRCHBAUM: (JEWISH/GERMAN) Late seventies - early eighties. Known as NINETY-TWO in the park. Retired barber. Holocaust survivor. Still suffers from nightmares.

GODFREY CASH: (AFRICAN AMERICAN) Mid to late thirties. Chess hustler. Smart. Intellectual. Had a great education. He wears glasses. Dresses in preppy clothing. Suffers from chronic back pain.

JEROME GUERRERO: (COMANCHE) 55 to 65 years old. Centered, but quick to anger. Dresses in jeans, a cowboy shirt, a brown cowboy hat, boots, and native jewelry.

JOHN ZHUK: (BELARUSIAN) Chess hustler. Mid to Late Thirties. Super emotional. Goes from zero to one hundred on his emotional speedometer. He's slovenly and wears cheap brand sweat pants and a sleeveless undershirt. Very religious.

PLACE:

Washington Square Park Chess Tables

SETTING:

The set is composed of two cement chess tables. For clarity, one table will be called *John's table*, and the other *Jerome's table*. Each table has two wooden benches where four people can sit comfortably. The benches are sturdy but worn out from overuse and weather. There's a two-foot walkway behind each table. There's a thick cement wall about two and a half to three feet in height after the walkway, where people can sit to watch the chess games. Discolored shrubbery is scattered behind the cement blocks. A handful of wildflowers grow in the shrubbery. An old bench and a water fountain round out the set.

TIME:

PRESENT. THE PLAY ALSO RUNS IN "REAL TIME."

PRODUCTIONS

Goodman/Teatro Vista Production – Cast and Crew

**(8 *character version*)

Rey Reyes – Raúl Castillo
Adam Kirchbaum - AKA - Ninety-Two – Howard Witt
Godfrey Cash – Cedric Mays
John Zhuk - Mike Cherry
Jerome Guerrero – Ricardo Gutierrez
Stuart – Daniel Cantor
Dr. Lee – Gordon Chow
Peewee – Kenn E. Head

Director – Edward Torres
Set Design – Collette Pollard
Lighting Design – Jesse Klug
Costume Design – Christine Pascual
Sound Design – Mikhail Fiksel
Graphics and Video design – John Boesche
Dramaturgs – Tanya Palmer, Kristin Leahey
Production Stage Manager – Kimberly Osgood

INTAR Theater Production – Cast and Crew

**(5 *character version*)

Rey Reyes – José Joaquín Pérez
Adam Kirchbaum - AKA - Ninety-Two – Ed Setrakian
Godfrey Cash – Shawn Randall
John Zhuk – Gardiner Comfort
Jerome Guerrero – David Anzuelo

Director - Lou Moreno
Set Design – Raul Abrego
Lighting Design – Christopher J. Cancel Pomales
Costume Design – Meghan E. Healey
Sound Design - Jesse Mandapat
Production Manager - Christopher J. Cancel Pomales
Production Stage Manager – Fran Acuña-Almiron
Assistant Stage Manager – Alejandra Maldonado Morales

ACT 1

In the darkness, we hear the loud ticking of a clock. After a few moments the banging of chess pieces on a chess table overtakes the ticking of the clock.

Lights rise at the chess tables in Washington Square Park. Cash and John sit at John's chess table, playing a blitz chess game. Cash plays with the black pieces - John with the white pieces. They play at a fast and furious pace, starting from move one to move fifteen. Jerome is playing chess by himself at his chess table. Ninety-Two sits at a park bench, asleep.

CHESS GAME #1
"Yum Yum"
{White-John} – {Black-Cash}

1. e2-e4 c7-c5 2. Nf1-Nf3 d7-d6 3. d2-d4 c5xd4 4. Nf3xd4 Nf8-f6 5.Nb1-c3 a7-a6 6. Bc1-e3 Nf6-g4 7. Be3-g5 h7-h6 8. Bg5-h4 g7-g5 9. Bh4-g3 Bf8-g7 10. h2-h3 Ng4-e5 11. Qd1-d2 Nb8-c6 12. O-O-O O-O (castles) 13. Nd4-f5 Bc8xf5 14. e4xf5 Qd8-a5 15. Kc1-b1 Ra8-c8 16. f2-f4 g5xf4. 17. Bg3-f4 Nc6-b4 18. Bxh6 Rc8xc3 19. Qd2-g5 Qa5xa2 + (check)

> Move played:
> Cash [B] - 15… Rook a8-c8.

CASH: I'm coming for your King. Come out. Come out. Where ever you are.

JOHN: You got nothing. I get to your King before you get mines. Open legs. Boom.

>Move played:
>John [W] - 16. f2-f4

CASH: You make me laugh with the baby moves.

>Move played:
>Cash [B] - 16. g5xf4

JOHN: Laugh now, brown cow.

>Move played:
>John [W] - 17. Bg3xf4

CASH: I hope you're not calling me a brown cow because I'm melanated. Because *that* would be racist. Let me bring another piece into the attack.

>Move played:
>Cash [B] - 17. Nc6-b4

JOHN: You Black and playing black pieces. Cash, you double black. (*Laughs.*) Now your King more dead than dead cow.

>Move played:
>John [W] - 18. Bf4xh6

CASH: Give me that good Knight. Yum, yum give me some.

>Move played:
>Cash [B] - 18. Rc8xNc3

JOHN: Take Knight. Knight is nothing. Mate in one.

> Move played:
> John [W] - 19. Qd2 g5

CASH: Forgive them, Lord, for they cannot see. You have a mate in one, and I mate in two. But it's my move. Therefore, I'll be mating first.

> Move played:
> Cash [B] - 19. Qxa2

CASH: CHECK! The moment of reckoning is upon you.

JOHN: Shit! (Distressed.) Draw?

CASH: Now that you're finally seeing the light, you're going to humiliate yourself and beg for a draw?

JOHN: No begging—friendly asking. Draw?

CASH: Jerome, you hear this man begging for a draw? He should be ashamed of himself.

JEROME: Maybe you should accept it.

CASH: Let me see if I understand what you're saying. I'm about to snuff the living daylights out of this manbaby, but you would like me to forgive him and let him live?

JOHN: Bible say, "Love prosper when debt forgiven."

JEROME: A draw is a fair outcome. No winner! No loser! Both sides get to walk away—happily, or unhappily. But at least they walk away.

CASH: I don't know what world you think you live in. Obviously not the one I happen to be inhabiting at the moment. It's all about the winning.

JEROME: Imagine this: two countries in the middle of a brutal, unnecessary war, on the verge of nuking each other into oblivion—call it a draw, shake hands, pack it up, go home, and start negotiating from anew? Think about it. The concept of a draw is genius. The draw can save humanity!

JOHN: I spit on draw.

JEROME: But you just asked for one.

JOHN: 'Cause I'm losing. Only beg when throat to get cut. (*To Cash, smiling meekly.*) Draw?

CASH: You're out of luck, my friend. The governor will not stay this execution. Make your move.

JOHN: I resign. Stupid game.

CASH: I see you came to your senses. Jerome, draws don't allow money to be exchanged. We're here to make a living.

JOHN: We no Mother Teresa, understand? Better to make money, too.

Yesterday, I pay bookie. Not everything, but lot. He say, if I don't pay everything today, him breaking hand. Yury like breaking hand because he say, "I put money in your hand, but your hand not put money in my hand, so I break your hand, 'cause your hand very bad hand. And broken hand not bad hand." I protest to him. Yury, my hand money-maker. I cannot pay back if you break hand. He laughed and say, "play with foot." I laugh, too. Pretty funny. Play with foot. Then he say, "I break foot too if foot don't put money in my hand." I better make money today. For Yury. Imagine me playing chess with foot! Cash here to make money, too. Cash son birthday tomorrow. Right, Cash?

CASH: Why are you bringing that up? That's why you're not invited to his party. And, it isn't as if his mother doesn't remind me enough. She *only* called me five times today. He wants a bike. And he doesn't want one of those fifty-dollar bikes either. He wants a Minnesota 1.0 Fat Bike. A thousand-plus dollars! I promised it to him last year, but… I better get it for him. Yesterday, I put some money down on one, but I'm still short. And today, I haven't lured one fish. Not one! Every day fewer and fewer fish come around. It gets harder and harder to make a living out here. And, to make matters worse, my back has been acting up all day! Damn, if everything doesn't come at you at once! (*To no one in particular.*) I NEED A PLAYER! NO EXPERIENCE NECESSARY!

JEROME: I was wondering why two hustlers would be playing against each other. Is this one of those desperate times call for desperate measures' situation?

CASH: Nah, nah, that was just a friendly game. To keep the blood flowing, you know? Hustlers don't hustle hustlers.

JOHN: When real fish come 'round, we ready for fight.

JEROME: But you guys made out like bandits yesterday. You beat the hell out of that poor guy, Bernie.

CASH: Not exactly like bandits. His pockets were full of air, if you get my drift. I need ten Bernies just to get out of these deep waters I find myself in.

JEROME: Beating a man like that was sad to see if you ask me. Not a good look on you guys.

JOHN: Nobody ask you.

CASH: Desperate times call for desperate measures. (*Winks and smiles at Jerome.*)

> *Cash opens a newspaper to the crossword puzzle and sits on the wall behind John's table. John pulls out horse racing forms from his Bible and studies them. Jerome sweeps around his table.*

JOHN: Fucking Jerome, stop with sweeping. Blowing dust in race forms.

JEROME: (*Jerome stops, looks at John as if saying, "Who cares?" then resumes sweeping.*) All those horses do is to take your money.

JOHN: Jeromes wrong like always. I got winner for race today. His name Salvation. I keep my form here in Psalm 23:1. "The Lord is my Shepherd, and I shall not want." Not want? Not want? I want. I want to win. Win. AND THIS MOTHERFUCKER KEEP WITH SWEEPING.

CASH: John, can you keep it down? It's too hot out here for all this commotion. Jerome, please!

> *Jerome stops sweeping and glares at John. John sets the chess pieces to their starting position.*

JOHN: You got point. It's hotter than devil armpit! Worse than to be virgin. One day earth kaput!

JEROME: Earth isn't going anywhere. Perhaps, man will become extinct, but the earth will continue on her merry way, circling the sun the way she's been doing for billions of years. Man can't see that our stay on earth is short lived.

CASH: You ever noticed when Jerome opens his mouth, he's usually on point. Not like some other people I know.

JOHN: Babaghanouj coming out Jeromes mouth.

JEROME: If you just shut your mouths for a second, and listen, you will hear mankind's clock winding down, signaling mankind's inevitable and most deserving end. And once the time runs out, it cannot be rewound. Tick... Tock... Tick... Tock.

JOHN: Read Revelation, you fucks. End of time. When Four Horsemen of Apocalypse ride up to you, throw stinking ass to ground, pray for mercy. God bringing pain. Kaput! Kaput!

CASH: There are Four Horsemen of the Apocalypse, and there are four horses in chess. Coincidence? I think not!

JOHN: Don't joke. Your rat ass eternity at stake!

CASH: Dag, it's slow out here! John, why don't you pray for some fish to come around?

JOHN: Good idea, mister. (*Folds hands in prayer.*) God, please, rain fish on your poor servant over here.

CASH: Is that what you call prayer? Anyway, I'm just going to sit here quietly and finish this crossword puzzle until fish start falling from the sky. (*Reads clue from crossword.*) Seven letters. Clue - will to live.

> *John goes back to his racing forms. Jerome cleans his chess pieces with a small rag. Rey Reyes enters carrying a briefcase while talking on his cell phone.*

REY: I'm not going home!... Not yet!... Maritza!... Please, listen to me. Just listen. You know what they did to him, right? They need to be taught a lesson... (*He stops, steals a glance at the hustlers, then drinks from the water fountain.*) Yes, I'm going to teach it to them. They can't go ripping off an old drunk man for all he's got... I know all they do is play chess all day. I did that once, too... I know, I haven't been playing lately, but... Hustlers can be hustled!... Yes, I'm going to hustle them... I don't have a problem. I don't... I'm not addicted. Besides, this isn't gambling. It's payback... If I lose, I lose. But I'm not going to lose... I know I've said that before... Why are you bringing up Guatemala? This has nothing to do with that... You don't trust me anymore? Okay, got to go! You know what, Maritza—losing is one of those things I know how to deal with... I have to go. (*He hangs up and takes another drink from the water fountain.*)

CASH: John, John, fish at water fountain!

JOHN: Thank God for God. He answer prayer.

CASH: Let's be cool. Maintain a sense of decorum. But let's not let him get away. And remember, I saw him first.

JOHN: Is not who see him first but who dinner plate he land in.

> *Cash and John surround Rey at the water fountain.*

JOHN: You look like chess player, play me couple, grasshopper.

CASH: John, what did I say? (*To Rey.*) Are you looking for a game? If you are and would like to play the best, you've found him. You speak Spanish? Yo hablo español. Quieres jugar conmigo? Tu eres Mexicano? Puertorriqueño? Cubano? Dominicano?

REY: I'm Guatemalan—Mayan. Half Mayan...

JOHN: Only language in world. Chess!

CASH: My friend here is monolingual. But, I use whatever tools I possess to bring in business. I speak a little German for my German customers - Danke. Swahili – Asante. Russian - Splecibo. French - Oui Oui. Italian - Buon Giorno! Chinese - Xie Xie. And Hillbilly - Y'all come back now! You name it, I speak it.

JOHN: One day all language in world dead. Bury. People only talk chess. E4 - Hello. Mate - Goodbye. Come talk a little chess with me, grasshopper.

CASH: Don't pay him any mind. You can deal with me. So, do you play or what?

REY: I'm not here to play. I'm looking for Stuart. Is he around?

JOHN: I Stuart.

CASH: No, he's not. Stuart might or might not come around today. Very unpredictable. Earlier, I bumped into one of our favorite fish, Dr. Lee, who informed me that Stuart was furious at us and might not ever come to the park again.

JOHN: Mad, for what?

CASH: I have no idea. You know, Stuart-- everything bothers him. We take his money. He becomes enraged. We don't take his money. He fumes. We take someone else's money. He explodes. You never know with Stuart. He's as unpredictable as the weather. He just might walk into the park whistling a happy tune. Whom should I say came looking for him?

REY: Oh, I'm Rey. Rey Reyes.

CASH: I don't mean to be intrusive, but can I inquire as to why you're looking for him?

REY: Came to repay a small loan.

JOHN: Give to me. I hold for him.

CASH: Where are my manners? I've been around with this social misfit for too long. I'm Godfrey Cash, but the world knows me as Cash. I got the fastest hands in the East. And, that's Russian John.

JOHN: Belarusian!

REY: Belarusian John?

JOHN: John. Just John.

REY: You guys are hustlers, right?

JOHN: He call us "H" word.

CASH: I'm more like a chess professor. Did you know it's easier to earn a doctorate degree than to become a chess grandmaster? How many taxi drivers have doctorates? Most of them! But how many are chess grandmasters?

REY: But you do play for money.

CASH: Just to make it interesting. Like sprinkles on ice cream.

REY: I'm Bernie's nephew.

CASH: Bernie? Is that the guy we played yesterday? That Bernie?

REY: Yeah, the guy you guys skinned alive.

CASH: That's such a harsh term - skinned alive. We only beat him for a few dollars.

JOHN: Beat him for nothing.

REY: Not only did you beat him for his paycheck, but he also had to borrow money from Stuart when he couldn't cover his losses. I call that skinned alive.

CASH: You say tomate. (*Spanish pronunciation.*) And I say tomato.

REY: (*Rey glances at his watch.*) Are you sure Stuart isn't going to come around today? I can come back another day. Maybe next week.

CASH: Look, he usually comes around with his grim-looking mug when it gets a little cooler—as the sun begins to set. (Looks at sky.) Just a few hours from now.

REY: I don't think I can wait that long.

CASH: Sometimes he comes earlier. You never know. Like I said, Stuart's unpredictable. Maybe today will be one of those days.

REY: I hope so. I can only wait for a few minutes.

CASH: So, now that that's settled, are you sure you don't want to play a few while you wait?

JOHN: Grasshopper, don't forget about your friendly Belarusian here.

REY: I think I'll pass. Besides, I promised my girl I wasn't going to gamble anymore.

Cash and John sensing an opening go at him.

CASH: Oh, so you're a gambling man!

JOHN: Like me. You play horses?

REY: No, no, no. Not a gambler—anymore!

CASH: Once a gambler, always a gambler. Am I right? Ah?

REY: Yeah, no. I mean… I have to stay on the straight and narrow. For her! You know how it is.

CASH: Actually, legally speaking, betting on chess games isn't considered gambling because it's a game of skill, not of chance.

REY: So, I wouldn't be gambling if I played chess for money?

JOHN: You very smart man. Brilliant! You genius with penis.

REY: Try explaining to my girl that it isn't gambling. I'm sorry.

Jerome walks over to them.

JEROME: Would you leave the man alone? He said he didn't want to play.

JOHN: Jeromes mind your business.

JEROME: Hi, I'm Jerome Guerrero.

REY: Rey Reyes.

JEROME: I heard. You're Mayan. I'm Comanche. We come from good people.

REY: But your name—Guerrero.

JEROME: My great-great grandfather wasn't trying to lose his scalp, so he took a Mexican surname. And it worked because—here I am! And I speak real Spanish. Not like – (*Points at Cash.*)

CASH: I speak impeccable Spanish.

JEROME: Yeah, okay. Keep believing that. (*To Rey.*) Why don't you come to my table? Sit in the cool shade. Relax a bit. Una partida entre amigos. Si?

REY: Are you a hustler, too?

JEROME: Yo? No! Mine is only a social game, you know, friendly. Not like—them. They see chess as a game of war. So tired of that dim-witted metaphor. Chess is so much more than that. For me, chess is a conversation between great minds where the search for truth and beauty is never ending. Would you like to have a little conversation with me?

REY: I don't know. I promised my girl I wasn't going to play.

JEROME: One friendly game? Ah?

JOHN: Jeromes go to your fucking table.

CASH: Jerome, Rey stated clearly that he didn't want to play with you.

REY: (*Rey takes notice of the hustlers' agitation and decides to play with Jerome.*) On second thought, I'll play you a game. A friendly game.

JEROME: That's what I'm talking about! Make your way to my table, young warrior.

Rey and Jerome walk to Jerome's table.

JOHN: Cash, you believe that?

CASH: Rey, when you want a good game, you know where to find me.

REY: (*To Jerome.*) No matter where I've lived—San Francisco, Chicago, Miami, Houston—this park—*Washington Square Park*'s chess tables was what chess players talked about. I can't believe I'm here.

JEROME: You moved around a lot. (*Rey takes it in but doesn't respond.*) Truth be told, this park has seen better days. I'm not going to delve into that subject, much less now that I have a game. I want to stay positive. In my view, mind you, this is a sacred place for those of us who like to make these chess pieces dance. And I don't mess with sacred places especially in the way they desecrated some of ours. Look at what they did to the sacred Black Hills. Four ungodly dead presidents faces carved on them, defiling those holy mountains. But that's a topic for another time. Look, people of all stripes come to this park to play this game. Look at right here. Everyone is a different race—different nationalities. You probably wouldn't find this diversity in another segment of our society. And, no one would believe you if you told them because people only seem comfortable in their closed-minded communities that conform to some sort of uniformity. This park is a coral reef for chess players. Chess brings us all together for better or worse. No more talking. Time to converse through chess. (*Jerome and Rey begin to play.*)

> Moves played:
> Jerome [W] - 1 .d2-d4
> Rey [B] - 1. d7-d5

JEROME: Okay. You want to go into the Queen's Gambit.

REY: What's that?

JEROME: You'll find out soon enough.

> Move played:
> Jerome [W] - 2. c2-c4

JEROME: That's the Queen's Gambit.

> Move played:
> Rey [B] - 2. d5xc4

JEROME: You accepted the gambit. Brave man. I love the subject matter of our chess conversation.

> Move played:
> Jerome [W] – 3. e2-e4

Ninety-Two lets out a loud scream that jolts Rey, but no one else overreacts.

JOHN: Damn! There go him again.

CASH: (*Cash, sees an opening to get Rey from Jerome's grasp.*) Jerome, can you take care of him? Please, you're the only one who can handle him.

JEROME: Why does he have to act up the very moment I have a game?

Ninety-Two let's out another scream.

CASH: Jerome, please!

JEROME: All right! All right! I'm going. Rey, please, give me a minute.

REY: No problem.

JEROME: I will be right back. (*He rushes over to Ninety-Two. Speaking softly.*) Wake up... Wake up.

NINETY-TWO: NOO! NOO!

JEROME: It's okay. You're in the park. You're safe.

NINETY-TWO: (*Opening eyes.*) Ah? Jerome! Thank God, it's you. Didn't I ask you not to let me fall asleep? Dear God. Why do we need to sleep?

JEROME: A man needs his rest.

NINETY-TWO: I can rest after I die.

JEROME: Come drink some water.

Jerome walks him to the water fountain.

NINETY-TWO: It's like I live in two worlds, this and... I don't ever want to sleep again. Never.

JEROME: That's nonsense. Drink! Drink!

NINETY-TWO: Same nightmare. Tall chimneys were chasing me. And, the more I ran from them the closer they got. Then, I fell in a garden full of blossoming… (*He checks his shirt pocket.*) My flower! My flower! Where is it? I had it in my pocket.

JEROME: It must've fallen out.

NINETY-TWO: I have to find it! Help me look for it, Jerome. I can't lose that flower.

> *They go back to the bench and look for the flower.*

JEROME: Check your hat. Don't want to go in a wild goose chase for nothing like last time.

NINETY-TWO: (*Ninety-Two checks hat.*) See? Nothing! Where could it be? (*To Cash and John.*) Did you guys see it?

CASH: No, I haven't.

> *John shakes head no.*

JEROME: Okay, relax. Do you remember the last time you had it?

NINETY-TWO: I don't know. I don't remember… I think it was by the card tables. I was showing it to a botany student. He was so impressed, he took a picture of it. Wanted to show his professor… I thought I put it back in my pocket… Take me there.

JEROME: Are you sure? Look, I'm in the middle of a game, and I don't want to go over there if you're not sure that's where you might've lost it.

NINETY-TWO: I don't know. I could've dropped it on my way back here. I got to retrace my steps. Take me there.

JEROME: No, no. I'll go. I could walk there faster by myself. You wait right here.

NINETY-TWO: No, I'm going with you. I can't lose that flower, Jerome.

JEROME: Come on then. Hurry! (*To Rey.*) Rey, don't go anywhere. I'll be right back. Okay?

REY: Yeah, okay.

> *Jerome and Ninety-Two exit. Cash and John rush over to Rey, feigning interest in the game on the chessboard. Last chance to reel him in.*

CASH: Very interesting game.

JOHN: Yes, very interesting.

REY: He lost a flower?

CASH: Actually, he's had it for so long it isn't a flower anymore. It's been reduced to powder.

JOHN: He think flower magical. Like bad thing don't happen to him because of flower.

CASH: Ninety-Two claims one day he was being held up at gunpoint. He brandished the "flower," scaring the mugger away.

REY: Ninety-Two?

CASH: It's what everyone calls him. Nickname, you know.

JOHN: They call him that because he fucking ninety-two years old.

CASH: Wrong! It's because he lives on 92nd Street. Ninety-Two was a child chess prodigy. He played against the greats of the time. Alexander Alekhine, Emmanuel Lasker, and even Jose Raul Capablanca, whom he beat!

REY: He played against them? Wow! I mean, those are the chess gods.

JOHN: Bullshit. I don't believe nothing old people say. Make up story all the time.

CASH: I looked at an old German newspaper, The Berliner Tageblatt. There was a photo of Ninety-Two as a kid playing Capablanca in a simultaneous exhibition. He wasn't lying.

JOHN: Because Cash studying for PhD, he think he know everything.

CASH: I do my research, okay?

JOHN: Cash so smart he drop out. And, they write about this motherfucker in magazine because he so smart. He even got chess games publish.

CASH: He thinks dropping out from a Ph.D. program is comparable to dropping out from middle school as he did.

JOHN: My book, dropping out is dropping out.

CASH: And, in my book, an ex-con is an ex-con!

JOHN: Ex. motherfucker!

CASH: He got arrested for breaking into a house. Guess what he stole. A chess book!

JOHN: You very stupid. I jewelry thief. One day, I broke into house. Saw expensive ass chess set. Understand? Chess book next to chess set. I open book and it was like Moses when red sea split open. I start to read book. Asshole owners came home and call cops. Understand?

CASH: It states clearly in that Bible of yours, "Thou shall not steal?" It would help if you read it sometime.

JOHN: Shut up, drop out.

CASH: Tell Rey how you escaped jail time. Listen to this.

JOHN: I told judge, I found chess! And, I wanted to play chess rest of my rat ass life. And, asshole judge love chess, too, and let me go. The judge come out to here to play me for few dollars a game. Last year he kaput. Miss taking asshole money.

CASH: If I were the judge, I would've given you the maximum sentence without the possibility of parole.

JOHN: But drop out can't be judge. Asshole drop out last motherfucking year. Why? For to be chess hustler? (*Laughs.*)

CASH: We have a comedian here, folks!

JOHN: Dropping out doctorate worse than stealing chess book. (*He laughs.*) I call you, Almost Dr. Cash now.

CASH: Rey, as you've noticed, it is impossible to have a serious discussion around here. And, because of that impossibility, you and I should play a few games.

REY: I'm in the middle of a game with Jerome.

CASH: I appreciate that you're a man of your word and all, but Jerome might be gone for a while. It isn't easy to find lost things in this park.

REY: I don't know, especially after what you did to my uncle yesterday.

JOHN: (*To Rey.*) What? You scare little girl? Wetting your panties? I be your pimp! I buy nice, short dress you wear in Christopher Street with fishnet stockings!

CASH: John, you can't get players by insulting them.

JOHN: Some flies like sugar. Some flies like shit. Sugar no work. Give them shit. (*To Rey.*) Garbage. You garbage. I sweep floor with your rat ass. Piece of shit! Dog shit! Horse shit! Elephant shit! No good piece of garbage shit. (*Nicely.*) Come play!

CASH: John! Be cool.

JOHN: I cooler than polar bear ass in Siberia ice storm! (*John walks to his table.*)

CASH: I apologize for my friend there. He's a philistine.

JOHN: Belarusian! Belarusian!

CASH: Today must be your lucky day, Rey. I'm going to give you the Cash discount.

REY: (*Rey looks at his watch.*) I don't have much time.

CASH: Time? Does time really exist? The only thing we have is the here and now! And right now, you're here, and I'm here. What are the chances that at this exact moment in time we find ourselves only a few feet apart in this vast, infinite universe? Astronomical! Yet, here we are, only a few feet away.

JOHN: Deep shit, Cash.

CASH: Look, I bet you want to be a good chess player. Am I right? But, you can only improve by playing with stronger players.

REY: I don't know. I do want to improve. I've done everything to get better. But, nothing's worked. I play with my computer, but I never beat it.

CASH: Even the strongest players in the world have trouble beating the chess program on their phones. Don't let that bother you.

REY: Maybe you're right. I just need to play tougher competition. I only play Bernie and you see how weak he plays.

CASH: He got a little game.

REY: Now, you're trying to make a fool out of me. Bernie can't play worth a dime. I even know that.

CASH: The issue here isn't Bernie. The issue here is whether you want to play or not. It's simple. If you don't, I can just go back to my crossword puzzle. It's up to you.

REY: *(Rey looks at his watch.)* I have to be leaving soon. But I'd love to get a couple of games in before I do. I hope Jerome doesn't mind.

JOHN: He don't mind, mister. Right, Cash?

CASH: He isn't here.

REY: Okay, but if I'm going to play someone, it might as well be the best in the park. The one I can learn the most from!

JOHN: Me. Sit down, sir.

CASH: Who is the only man in this park who takes on all comers? Moi! I don't care if it's a world-class grandmaster. I fear no man. Can anyone else make that claim? Didn't think so! See how quiet he got?

REY: So, I guess it's you then.

CASH: Hey, John, let me use your table.

JOHN: Go ahead. But I want side bet.

REY: Side bet?

CASH: You know. You bet against both of us.

REY: What? So, it's me against the two of you.

JOHN: Rat scum, you using my table and pieces, too?

CASH: I think it's the fair thing to do.

REY: ...Okay, okay. Let's try a few.

CASH: John, can I use your clock?

JOHN: You break, you pay.

> *Cash sits at John's table. John hands Cash chess clock.*

CASH: Thank you. You're a gentleman and a scholar! Come, Rey, sit. Sit.

> *Rey sits at John's table across from Cash as he sets up the chess clock.*

CASH: Okay, my office is now open. I'm giving you the Cash Special. I'm only giving myself three minutes and I'm giving you five. I'm only doing it because you seem like a good citizen. Are you ready?

REY: So, what we're playing for? Two dollars a game?

CASH: For two dollars, you couldn't get the time of day out of me. Twenty a game!

REY: Twenty? That's a little too steep.

CASH: Rey, you're playing the top of the line here. You expect to pay a little more for fillet mignon than for chuck steak, right? Don't you pay more for a Broadway show than for one of those funky shows in the Village no one understands? And you expect to pay a whole lot more for caviar than for deviled ham spread. Top of the line requires a more significant financial investment.

REY: Let me get this straight. So, I'd be betting twenty dollars against each of you?

CASH: You got it, Sherlock.

REY: I don't know. I mean, I'll lose forty dollars every time I lose a game.

JOHN: And, you win forty every time you win. Understand?

REY: I don't know.

CASH: You know what? Get the hell away from the table! I don't have time to waste with you. Play or don't play, but don't jerk me around.

REY: I don't mean to get you upset, but…
Okay… Let's play a couple.

CASH: Why do must I get upset to get a chess game around here?

REY: I'm sorry.

CASH: Let bygones be bygones. Let's just play. Do you know how to use the clock?

REY: …Yeah.

CASH: Good! So, start my clock!

CHESS GAME #2
"Father Issues"
[White-Cash] [Black- Rey]

1. e2-e4 b7-b6 2. f2-f4 Bc8-b7 3. Nb1-c3 g7-g6 4. Ng1-f3 Bf8-g7 5. d2-d4 d7-d6 6. Bf1-d3 e7-e6 7. f4-f5 g6xf5 8. e4xf5 e6-e5 9. d4xe5 d6xe5 10. Bd3-b5+ Nb8-d7 11. Bc1-g5 f7-f6 12. Nf3xe5 c7-c6 13. Qd-h5 Ke8-e7 14. Qh5-f7+ Ke7-d6 15. 0-0-0+ Kd6-c5 16. Qf7-c4 Mate

The moves will get played throughout the scene. Rey hesitantly hits the clock. Cash confidently makes the first move. Rey clumsily makes a move knocking a few pieces down.

REY: Sorry.

CASH: No need to apologize. Just fix them.

Rey fixes the pieces.

JOHN: Cash, we should put five-dollar limit on every table in park. Throw Jeromes ass out. He got best table in park. Under tree. And don't play for money.

CASH: I don't want anyone bothering him today. Things are bad enough already. And you know how touchy Jerome is about his table.

JOHN: Fuck Jeromes. He no scare me.

CASH: Damn it! Here he comes. Don't start anything.

Jerome and Ninety-Two, holding a small plastic transparent bag in his hand, enter. Jerome leads Ninety-Two to his table.

NINETY-TWO: Thank God I found it! This flower has protected me for such a long time. I wouldn't know what I would do if I lost it.

JEROME: It doesn't protect you from your nightmares.

NINETY-TWO: Even this flower has its limits.

JEROME: (*Jerome notices Rey playing Cash.*) Will you look at that? They snatched up my player.

NINETY-TWO: I'm sorry, Jerome. It's my fault.

JEROME: Hey, Rey, couldn't wait five minutes?

CASH: He's just playing me a few games. You will have him back in no time.

JEROME: I was talking to Rey.

REY: I'm sorry. But I'm just playing them a couple of games, then we could finish our game.

JEROME: I'll be waiting.

JOHN: Jeromes, we putting five-dollar charge minimum on every table in park. Go to Central Park to play for free!

CASH: Why John? Why? Why are you going to start with Jerome?

JEROME: This park belongs to all the human beings on this planet, not just to you. As a matter of fact, you shouldn't even be allowed to walk in the park since you still haven't mastered the art of being a human being. Maybe, you've mastered the art of being a primate but not of a human being.

JOHN: What fuck Jeromes say? Don't understand fuck.

JEROME: You act more like a monkey than a human. That's what I said. Understand me now?

JOHN: Monkey? I no monkey, mister! You messing with our money. Right, Cash?

CASH: John, what did I tell you?

JEROME: Do you really think you're going to push me out of the park the way you hustlers pushed out all the other social players? This is the last free table in the park, and it's going to stay that way. You're not taking over my table the way they stole my land.

JOHN: Stop with Indian land thing. Shit offend people.

JEROME: Let me get this straight. So, the fact that my people were the victims of a genocidal policy, which, if I may add, is still in effect today, doesn't offend *them*, but the fact that I mention it *does*? Ain't that some shit? Fuck them if they get offended! Goddamn it, I'm offended. (*To Ninety- Two.*) You see why I always have to bring it up? See the ignorance I'm up against? (*To everyone.*) I don't want people to forget that this continent was and will always be Indigenous land.

JOHN: How going to forget? You say it every day.

JEROME: Nobody listens. Everyone has a short memory, if they have any at all. You come to this country and act like we don't even exist.

JOHN: My father brung me to this country against my will. Just like Cash was brung here to work like slave against his will. Right, Cash?

CASH: Correction, my people were enslaved! A verb. Slave is a noun. Big difference.

JOHN: What difference?

JEROME: You were stolen from your land, and my people's land was stolen from us by people who won't take responsibility for their crimes against humanity. We're both homeless!

CASH: I'd love nothing more than to entertain this discussion, however, at the present moment I find myself preoccupied with the main reason I come to this park in the first place. And that is to make a living.

JOHN: Jeromes angry man.

JEROME: I wonder what's the reason for that is.

NINETY-TWO: Jerome, come here. Come. Sit. Sit.

> *Jerome goes to his table, but instead of sitting, he paces.*

NINETY-TWO: Jerome, ignore John. Everyone does. Don't let that schlepper bother you. He's just trying to get your goat. You're smarter than that.

JEROME: I don't want anyone going near my table, period!

NINETY-TWO: Hey, I'm on your side, my friend. Calm down. Get a drink of water.

> *Jerome reluctantly goes to the water fountain, but doesn't drink and returns to his table.*

JEROME: If you open just one page of a history book about my people and it doesn't enrage you, there's something seriously wrong with you. They can call me angry all they want. People come to me with "you're nothing like Indians in the movies— full of wisdom." I say to them, "That's right I'm no stereotype. I don't dance with wolves, you brainless ass." Come at me right or don't come at me at all.

NINETY-TWO: You have every right to feel and express yourself however you please. I just don't want you to blow a gasket and get a heart attack trying to educate the ignorant amongst us. Don't want to lose you over stupid crap.

> *Jerome laughs and Ninety-Two joins him.*

JEROME: You got a point there, my friend. I don't want my tombstone to read, "He died arguing with morons." (*They laugh.*)

NINETY-TWO: No one deserves that.

JEROME: You are wise beyond your years. (*They laugh.*)

NINETY-TWO: I wish that was true.

JEROME: What I miss most about my fishing boat is being in the middle of the ocean with my crew, away from the horde of nitwits, watching the stars, and eating fresh fish. (*Gets lost in the memory. Returns.*) Talking about fish. (*Points to Rey.*) You see that kid over there? That's Bernie's nephew. Goes by the name of Rey.

NINETY-TWO: Bernie? That poor schmuck from yesterday? Can he play?

JEROME: As good as Bernie. Correction—as bad as Bernie!

NINETY-TWO: Jerome, we got to get that kid away from them.

JEROME: The history of my nation has taught me not to get involved in other people's problems. My Nation got involved in the Revolutionary War, and we suffered from the wrath of the colonies. Then, we sided with the colonies in the War of 1812, and we still suffered from the wrath of the colonies. Better to stay clear from other people's messes. That's what I think.

NINETY-TWO: Introduce me!

JEROME: Why must you always interfere? You should let people work things out for themselves.

NINETY-TWO: Not everyone can. Sometimes people need a hand. Please, Jerome!

JEROME: You're always trying to help people in this park. Have you ever succeeded?

NINETY-TWO: It doesn't mean I'm going to stop trying. Some people are not even aware they need help. It's like fishing. You cast your line and hope the fish bites and doesn't squirm off the hook as you reel it in.

JEROME: Hope is an important part of fishing but it isn't enough. You must have the right bait.

NINETY-TWO: Here's hoping I do.

JEROME: You would've made a great fisherman, my friend. I could've used you on my boat.

NINETY-TWO: Introduce me. Look, after we pry him away, you can finish your game with him.

JEROME: As tempting as that sounds, I'm going to have to decline.

NINETY-TWO: Do it for me.

JEROME: I'm sorry. I don't want anything to do with them.

NINETY-TWO: I respect your point of view, but I can't just sit here and allow someone else to get taken advantage of in this park. I can't do it, Jerome.

JEROME: We all must follow our calling. But be careful, those two sharks are going to protect their prey with their lives.

NINETY-TWO: I got my flower to protect me.

JEROME: Go on then, great savior.

NINETY-TWO: Oh, no. Don't call me that. That's the furthest from the truth. My batting average is very low, below the Mendoza line.

> *Ninety-Two tries to walk to John's table, but John blocks his path.*

JOHN: Game going over here.

> *Ninety-Two puts flower by John's face.*

JOHN: Get flower away from face.

> *Ninety-Two gets by John.*

CASH: Not today, Ninety-Two.

NINETY-TWO: I just want to meet the kid. Hi! Rey? Right? It's a pleasure to meet you. Nice haircut! Must've paid a pretty penny for a cut like that. I used to be a barber, I know. I used to own a barbershop that catered to Wall Street professionals. I'm retired now, but I can still spot a great haircut. What do you do if you don't mind me asking?

REY: I'm a computer programmer for a bank in mid-town.

NINETY-TWO: My first thought was that he worked in a bank.

JOHN: Hey, Cash, Nine-Two read hairs. (*Laughs.*)

NINETY-TWO: I don't know anything about computers. I'm a dinosaur, I guess.

REY: Actually, it isn't that complicated. One of my jobs is to make sure that data isn't compromised during a transaction.

NINETY-TWO: You've lost me already. Jerome, smart kid.

REY: Let me put it like this. If you take out a hundred dollars from an ATM, you want the main computer to reflect the same amount. You don't want it to say that you took out a thousand. It's not that hard.

CASH: So, are the salutations over with? Because we have some business to take care of here.

REY: Cash told me you were a chess prodigy.

NINETY-TWO: A long time ago. In another lifetime.

REY: And, that you beat my favorite player, Jose Raul Capablanca.

NINETY-TWO: My favorite, too! Now that Cuban was a real child prodigy! He was the Mozart of Chess. His games were like symphonies. I beat him in a simultaneous exhibition. He was playing fifty of us. I just got lucky.

REY: Nobody ever got lucky against Capablanca. He didn't lose a single tournament game for ten years.

NINETY-TWO: I beat Alexander Alekhine, too. Superstitious! He had a black cat named Chess, and he made the poor cat walk across the chessboard before every single game. Crazy! But he was an attacking genius.

CASH: Okay, this history lesson is now over.

NINETY-TWO: Lasker was my coach.

REY: Emanuel Lasker? The champion?

NINETY-TWO: Is there another Emanuel Lasker? World Champion for twenty-seven years. He was a little guy but he was always smoking a huge cigar—bigger than him! The first player to use psychology against his opponents. Brilliant mind.

CASH: Stop it, Ninety-Two. I know what you're doing.

NINETY-TWO: What am I doing? I'm not doing anything. (*To Rey.*) When I was a kid, all those great players used to pass by Berlin every

79

now and then to play in tournaments or to give exhibitions.

CASH: Rey, are you ready?

REY: Yeah, yeah. I'd love to talk more about that Golden Era of Chess. It's my favorite.

NINETY-TWO: Mine too! Did you know that Lasker and Albert Einstein were the best of friends?

REY: Really?

CASH: Every time I get a player, Ninety-Two tries to wrest them away by telling them these antediluvian stories. Right, John? I've heard the Einstein – Lasker story so many times I memorized it. It goes like this. Einstein and Lasker were always arguing. (*Imitates Ninety-Two.*) Einstein would scream at Lasker: "Emanuel, you are wasting that brilliant mind of yours playing chess!" And then Lasker would yell back at Einstein how he wouldn't be able to prove the theory of relativity: "You won't be able to prove it, Albert. You won't be able to." How did I do, Ninety-Two?

NINETY-TWO: Don't be disrespectful. I'll put my foot up your tuchus.

CASH: Then, Ninety-Two laments about how he was never able to understand the theory of relativity. Maybe, if I explain it to you once and for all, you won't keep trying to steal my players. Einstein explained it like this. Pay close attention now. Put your hand on a hot stove for a minute, and it seems like an hour. Sit with a pretty girl for an hour, and it seems like a minute. That's relativity. Do you understand it now, Ninety-Two?

NINETY-TWO: Now, you're trying to ridicule me.

CASH: Ninety-Two, you're always interfering in our business.

NINETY-TWO: You're exaggerating.

CASH: You know, Ninety-Two, you should start playing chess again. That way, you'll be too busy to stick your nose in our business.

REY: You don't play chess? Why not?

NINETY-TWO: It's a long boring story.

CASH: Because he rather pester those of us that are out here trying to make a living. Now, Ninety-Two, you can excuse yourself and go talk to Jerome about the good old days in the park. Rey, pay attention to your game.

NINETY-TWO: Rey, you don't have to play. You can play Jerome just for fun. His pieces are eagerly awaiting you.

REY: I'll be there soon.

CASH: You heard the man. Goodbye, Ninety-Two! Walk away. Keep walking. Goodbye and good riddance.

Ninety-Two returns to Jerome's table.

> Move played:
> Cash [W] - 15. O-O-O+
> (Castles Queenside)

CASH: Check!

REY: (*Rey studies the chessboard.*) I don't know what to do.

CASH: You're getting mated in the next move.

REY: Then, I resign. I didn't see anything. Man, your pieces encircled my King like sharks in a feeding frenzy.

CASH: (*Cash quickly sets up his chess pieces.*) But you played well. Right, John?

JOHN: Not bad. Knight e7 interesting move.

JEROME: Beware of compliments spiked with arsenic.

CASH: Jerome, you are so paranoid.

JEROME: If my people had been more paranoid, we would've sent those pilgrims back to the hell they came from, and we'd still have our land. I'm just saying a little paranoia can sometimes save your life.

JOHN: And then we have no Thanksgiving Day. I like turkey, mister.

JEROME: Small price to pay not to be slaughtered. Anyway, you still have Columbus Day, don't you?

CASH: He said ironically!

JEROME: Funny how this country celebrates the demise of my people. I just want to point that out. Now, we can all go back to watch some mindless television programming.

CASH: Look, Jerome, we're just trying to help the kid.

JEROME: Oh yeah? By taking away his money?

CASH: (*To Rey.*) See, if you would've made a couple of different moves, you could've won.

JEROME: If my uncle had tits, he'd be my aunt.

REY: So, I'm not totally hopeless?

CASH: Just don't let your King get stuck in the center of the board.

JOHN: Very, very bad King in center. What, you don't like King, mister?

REY: I thought the center of the board was the safest place for him.

CASH: No, no. I must agree with John there. And that doesn't happen very often. When the King is in the center, he can be attacked from many different directions. You must get him out of the center as soon as possible and put him in the corner. You don't want to have a King without a castle. Chess players with father issues usually leave their Kings in the center of the board without protection.

NINETY-TWO: Bah, psychological mumbo jumbo.

JOHN: You got father issues? No problem. I hate my father, too.

CASH: John that keeps you from becoming a stronger player. See, when you lose, you're supposed to hurt so much, you don't want to experience that pain again, and that forces you to improve. However, when you lose, you relish in the vicarious feeling of seeing your father dead before you. You better reconcile your relationship with your father if you want to keep improving. I recommend the same for you, Señor Rey.

REY: It's too late for that. My father is dead.

CASH: Then, it's more important than ever.

REY: I can't believe you see all that by how I played. Amazing.

NINETY-TWO: Don't listen to that crap. You left your King in the center of the board because you didn't know what you were doing. Look, let me put it this way, leaving your King in the center is like a boxer using his face to block his opponent's punches. Sorry to hear about your father.

REY: No, no, don't be sorry. If my father had seen me walking down the street, he wouldn't have known who I was. Met him just before he died.

NINETY-TWO: It's tough growing up without a father. Mine was taken from me at a very early age. But, I had a mother who more than made up for it. I hope your mother was there for you.

REY: I wish! My mother died when I was six. I was raised by my uncle, Bernie. He was the one who taught me how the chess pieces moved.

NINETY-TWO: Some people don't even have an uncle. Consider yourself fortunate.

REY: Never thought about it like that.

NINETY-TWO: People get stuck on what they lack rather than appreciate what they have.

CASH: Come on. Pay up!

> *Rey pays the hustlers, then sets up his pieces.*

CASH: Ready for the next one?

REY: I don't know.

CASH: What is there to know?

REY: I'm down forty dollars. I'm overmatched. And, I still have to pay Stuart.

JOHN: You got big problem. You got no faith in you. Understand? You could win next game.

CASH: Okay, just one more. And because I have an abundance of generosity, I'm going to take another minute off my clock. I'm only going to have two minutes to play my whole game. That's really hard!

REY: I don't know.

CASH: Rey, you disappoint me. Are you a gambling man or what? Where would mankind be if it didn't take chances? I tell you where. Living in caves. Look at us! We go to the moon! Not always successfully, but we go. And one day, we'll be traveling to other galaxies because we take chances. I know—you know—what I'm talking about. I know you do.

REY: You got a point, but…

CASH: Look, you get the white pieces this time. You make the first move. You do know that white wins over fifty five percent of the games?

JOHN: Every time!

CASH: So, I'm starting the clock.

NINETY-TWO: Rey, you can walk away right now. You're only down a few dollars.

JEROME: Just come over here where playing a chess game won't cost you a dime.

REY: Um... (*Thinks about it.*) I'm going to try one more. Then, I'll stop. This time, you give me five minutes against your two. Right?

CASH: Right. But, it means that we'll be playing for forty dollars a game.

JOHN: Times two, mister.

CASH: Tell you what! Let's round it off and make it fifty a game.

REY: Fifty?

CASH: Yeah! I like big round numbers. They're easier to keep track of.

REY: But how did we go from twenties to fifties?

CASH: Let me explain it to you. When I take a minute off my clock, we also double the bet. I'm taking a bigger risk by having less time. So, you must take a risk too! Your risk is merely monetary. It's quite logical.

JOHN: Cash give you chess knowledge. You give us money. Good trade! Understand? And now, Cash only two minutes for play whole game. Two minutes—is nothing!

REY: Okay, let's play one more. If I play really fast, I might be able to win.

CASH: I'm going to start the clock. Fifty!

REY: Fifty? Okay. One more.

CHESS GAME #3
"Defective Brain"
[White- Rey] [Black- Cash]

1. e2-e4 d7-d5 2. f2-f4 d5xe4 3. d2-d3 Ng8-f6
4. h2-h3 e7-e5 5. Nb1-c3 Bf8-b4 6.f4xe5 Nf6-d5
7.Qd1-d2 Bb4xc3 8. b2xc3 e4-e3 9. Qd2-e2 Qd8-e4+ (Check) 10. Ke1-d1 Nd5xc3 mate

> *Rey takes off his jacket. Cash starts clock. Rey makes a move and hits the clock. Cash answers immediately. Several moves get played quickly.*

NINETY-TWO: They raised the stakes, Jerome. They got him now. They got him!

JEROME: There goes my game.

NINETY-TWO: Yeah, he's not getting off that table until his wallet is empty.

> *A bunch of moves get played. Cash doesn't even seem to be thinking as he moves quickly. Rey seems indecisive.*

> Move played:
> Cash [B] - 9. Qd8-h4+

CASH: Check!

REY: It's unbelievable how fast you are.

> Move played:
> Rey [W] - 10. Ke1-d1

Cash quickly makes his move.

>Move played:
>Cash [B] - 10. Nd5xc3

CASH: Mate! Pay up! (*Cash quickly sets up his pieces.*)

REY: I can't believe how badly I'm playing. My brain is defective. I'm better than this. (*Rey pays the Hustlers. His cell phone rings. He looks at the caller ID.*) I'm sorry. I have to take this. My girl!

CASH: Come on, Rey! Really?

REY: Sorry, but I have to. (*Rey walks to the water fountain for privacy.*)

CASH: Women!

REY: Hey... No, I'm still at the park... Still waiting for him to show up. He should be here any minute now. Yeah, I'm playing.... Not good! I'm just a little rusty, that's all. I'm improving every game... I'm only down a few games... Yes, down a few dollars...

CASH: Oil and vinegar. That's what chess and women are. Oil and vinegar.

NINETY-TWO: Women don't stand a chance once Caissa gets her hooks on you. The Chess Goddess is one hell of a demanding mistress. Beautiful, alluring, irresistible, Caissa.

REY: I'm playing Cash, the one who beat uncle Bernie. He's really good. Better than I expected. And super-fast! But I know I can beat him.

JOHN: Old girlfriend say, man that play chess very good is sign for wasted life. She call chess brain disease. Like tumor with cancer but worse.

REY: I can't stop now... No, it isn't my addiction talking...

CASH: At first women are impressed when they find out you play chess, then they get competitive with it, then comes the ultimatum—it's me or chess.

REY: Are you going to keep bringing up Guatemala? Of course, I feel fucked up, Maritza! How do you expect me to feel?

NINETY-TWO: The famous artist Marcel Duchamp, a strong player in his own right, spent the first week of his honeymoon studying chess. His wife was so fed up, she waited until he went to sleep and glued all the chess pieces to the board. Their marriage didn't last more than three months.

REY: I'm going to start winning now... Maritza, I have to go... I have to go... I'm hanging up! *(Rey ends the call and returns to the chess table.)*

JEROME: My wife and I play a chess game every night before we go to bed. It's relaxing.

NINETY-TWO: My wife, may she rest in peace, was always telling me to play. She could see how much I still loved the game. I regret not giving her the satisfaction of seeing me play.

REY: My girl doesn't want me to play. She made me sell an eight-hundred-dollar Staunton chess set. A four-hundred-dollar chess table! First-print chess books! I got like two hundred dollars for the whole thing, and it was worth thousands. She says chess brings out the worst in me.

CASH: God knows nobody loves women more than I do. And I can talk about them forever. God bless every single one of them, including my ex., but Rey, we have to finish what we started. Are you ready?

> *Rey is stopped by Ninety-Two as he walks to John's table.*

NINETY-TWO: Rey, quit before you fall further behind.

REY: I can't quit now. I'm down.

NINETY-TWO: Don't want you to end up like your uncle.

JOHN: There he go again.

CASH: You heard the man. He wants to play. Besides, I'm taking another minute off my clock. He gets five minutes, and I only get one. One! Your chances of winning multiply exponentially.

NINETY-TWO: Don't be a schmuck, Cash. He has no chance, even at those odds.

CASH: Ninety-Two remind me not to hire you as my publicist.

JOHN: If you play fast, you could beat him. Don't doubt you. This big boy chess. Understand? Man chess! He only one minute. Is nothing.

REY: Five to one? No disrespect, but I can't see you beating me with only a minute. (*Rey sits at John's table.*)

CASH: That's why we're playing for a hundred!

REY: A hundred?

CASH: Hey, I took another minute off my clock. We keep doubling, right? And, because I'm feeling magnanimous, I'm going to give you the white pieces again.

JOHN: You get white pieces again!

REY: Okay. Let's do it! I can win this one. I know it! (*Rey loosens his tie.*)

CHESS GAME #4
"Book Trap"
[White - Rey] [Black - Cash]

1.d2-d4 d7-d5 2.c2-c4 e7-e6 3.Nb1-c3 Bf8-e7 4.Bc1-d2 c7-c6 5.f2-f3 Qd8-d6 6.c4-c5 Be7-h4 + Check 7.g2-g3 Qd6xg3+ 8.h2xg3 Bh4xg3 Mate

Cash and Rey rattle off the first four moves. Rey hesitates before making his next move.

>Move played:
>Rey [W] - 5. f2-f3

CASH: You shouldn't have pushed your Bishop Pawn.

REY: Why not?

CASH: It opens your King position up for this tactical combination.

>Move played:
>Cash [B] - 6. Be7-h4+

Check!

>Move played:
>Rey [W] - 7. g2-g3

CASH: Now, I'll sack my Queen on g3. BAM!

>Move played:
>Cash [B] - 7. Qd6xg3+

CASH: You're forced to take back.

>Move played:
>Rey [W] - 8. h2xg3

CASH: Bishop takes g3.
>Move played:
>Cash [B] - 8. Bh4xg3

CASH: Mate!

JOHN: Damn, Cash you brilliant.

CASH: You're embarrassing me, John. As wonderful and true as that compliment is, how do you expect me to respond to it? You might not be able to tell but I'm blushing. All this winning has gotten me thirsty. (*Cash walks over to the water fountain.*)

REY: Wow, that's amazing.

JOHN: Man, that's nothing. It's book trap. Pay up!

> *Rey pays John and Cash. Rey takes off his tie and opens the top button of his shirt.*

REY: I can't believe this. You only had one minute. Come on, let's play another!

CASH: Relax, man. We have the rest of the day and night to play. (*Cash and John exchange looks. They have a fish on a hook.*)

REY: Let's go! Come on! Let's go. Let's play.

CASH: (*Cash walks back to John's table.*) Rey, I'm going to do you a favor. I'm going to give you a chance to win your money back. Even though it's against my best interest, I'm going to allow you to double the bet. Make it two hundred a game. Would you like that?

REY: I don't care. Let's do it.

CASH: Two hundred it is then. (*Cash starts the clock, and they rattle off a bunch of moves.*)

CHESS GAME #5
"Fuck Me"
[White - Cash] [Black - Rey]

1. e2-e4 e7-e5 2. Ng1-f3 Nb8-c6 3. Bf1-c4 Bf8-c5 4. b2-b4 Bc5-b4 5.c2-c3 Bb4-a5 6. O-O Ng8-e7 7. Nf3-g5 d7- d5 8. e4xd5 Nf6xd5 9. Ng5xf7 Ke8xf7 10.Qd1-f3+ Kf2-e6 11.Bc1-a3 Ba5-b6 12. Rf1-e1 Nc6-a5 13. Re1xe5+ Ke6xe5 14. g2-g4 g7-g6 15. d2-d4+ Ke5-e6. 16. Qf3-e4+ Ke6-f7 17. Bc4xd5+ Kf7-g7 18. Ba3-e7 Rh8-e8 19. Qe4-e5+ Kg7-h6 20. g4-g5+ Kh6-h5 21. Bd5-f3+ Bc8-g4 22. Qe5-g3 (+ *symbol means Check*)

NINETY-TWO: Stupid, stupid, stupid, stupid...

JEROME: How many times have we seen this?

NINETY-TWO: Too many! Too many!

JEROME: Remember what this park used to be back in the day? Every day was like a chess festival. On any given day, we had two or three Grandmasters playing out here. Even a champion used to stop by every now and then. Everyone played for fun. But, look at what we have now. Everything changed when the hustlers took over the tables and put a price tag on the game. I've been thinking. Maybe, they're right. Maybe, I should go to Central Park. At least I'll get some games there.

NINETY-TWO: They tell you this every day. Why start listening to them today?

JEROME: It's almost impossible to get a game here anymore. The more I think about it, the more sense it makes. I need to pack it up. Every day is some something with them. I just want to play my chess games and be left alone. Is that too much for a man to ask? Tell me if it is.

NINETY-TWO: No, my friend.

JEROME: Then, why should I keep coming down here, when I could play as many games as I want in Central Park? My chess crew, Camilla, The Arab, and Puerto Rican Joe, keep asking me when I'm going to join them. They're smart. When they saw the scene down here changing, they put two and two together, packed up their pieces, left, and never looked back. It's about time I do the same.

NINETY-TWO: What about me? Who's going to wake me from my nightmares? Who's going to assist me on my return to the world of the living?

JEROME: You're the reason I haven't left. Just come to Central Park with me. Huge Elm trees surround the chess tables blocking out the sun completely. Their shade makes it feels like the park has air conditioning. It's like being in an enchanted forest full of chess players. And, the best thing is that the tables are far away from the street noise. So quiet that you can actually hear your own thoughts.

NINETY-TWO: It's too big of a schlep to get there. It's dead center in the park. And, when you get there, you have to climb a hill to get to the tables.

JEROME: A small hill.

NINETY-TWO: No such thing as a small hill when you've reached my age. I'm too old to make that trek. I know one thing, Jerome, this place won't be the same without you. So, I'm begging you not to go.

At John's table.

CASH: Hey, Rey, think long, think wrong! Tick. Tick. Tick. You don't have to think that much. This is chess.

                  Move played:
                  Rey [B] -16. Ke6-f7

CASH: Look at that. You see this man? He's trying to bring his King to safety. See, a couple of lessons, and he's already trying to win. Don't improve too fast there. Give me that Knight.

                  Move played:
                  Cash [W] - 17. Bc4xd5+

CASH: Check!

REY: Fuck!

                  Move played:
                  Rey [B] - 17. Kf7-g7

CASH: Mind your French. How are you going to answer this move?

                  Move played:

Cash [W] - 26. Qe5-g3

CASH: Hey, look. (*Shows clock to Rey.*) You ran out of time. You lose.

REY: What?

CASH: You used up all of your time. That makes me upset because I had this beautiful mate, I was going to lay on you.

REY: FUCK ME! Fuck! I can't believe this... FUCK! My girl is going to go ballistic. (*Rey pays the hustlers.*)

CASH: Hey, don't take it so hard. Just go to an ATM and withdraw some money. Wait, don't tell me you don't have a bank account like your uncle. That's what he told us. That was the reason he had to borrow money from Stuart. He was speaking incoherently about how the Guatemalan government is going after him. And, he thinks the government can trace him if he has a bank account. Is that true, or was that the alcohol talking?

REY: He told you that? He never talks about it. I can't believe he told you. He isn't a criminal or anything like that. He was a witness to something... A massacre. But, they're not after him anymore. They never were. But in his mind... you know! Witnessing a massacre can fuck up your head!

NINETY-TWO: (*To Jerome.*) A massacre?

CASH: So, are you going to play or what?

JEROME: That is some cold shit. He just told you his uncle witnessed a massacre, and you guys don't blink an eye.

JOHN: Time is money, mister!

JEROME: Don't expect any sympathy from these guys.

CASH: That's the oldest trick in the world. The fish always comes up with some sappy story to try to get our sympathy when they lose. They either had a hard day at work—or their wives are busting their balls—or they're tired, hungry, or sleepy. We've heard them all before.

REY: I didn't know it was that obvious.

CASH: I'm trying to make a living out here. I don't have time for sympathy. So, are you going to play?

REY: Let me get a sip of water first. (*Rey walks to the water fountain taking a sip of water.*)

CASH: Be careful! Watering holes are some of the most dangerous places in the animal kingdom. Isn't that right, Jerome? Predators know that their potential meals are at their most vulnerable when drinking water. That's when they take their eyes off of them.

JEROME: Unless you are a crocodile. Then, the watering hole is your dining table.

CASH: Jerome, why do you have to be such a contrarian?

JEROME: I'm agreeing with you.

CASH: You just proved my point. (*Cash stretches his back. It's somewhat painful.*)

NINETY-TWO: Cash, could I have a word with you?

CASH: Sure, what is it, Ninety-Two?

NINETY-TWO: Could you please lay off the kid? That kid isn't like his uncle. Something isn't right about him. I see it in his eyes.

CASH: I tell you what. After I beat him one more game, I'll release him back into the ocean like a juvenile tuna.

JOHN: Nobody made him to play. Free country.

JEROME: This country hasn't been free for four hundred years!

NINETY-TWO: I thought you guys were better than that.

JEROME: Maybe, they're not.

NINETY-TWO: You know, Jerome, I wanted to give them the benefit of the doubt. But, you just might be right. YOU ARE A BUNCH OF GODDAMN PREDATORS!

CASH: I don't appreciate you calling me a predator. Let me explain to you why. This is my job. Any man that walks into this park knows what I am. I never deny nor conceal what I do for a living. Hence, not a predator. Predators go after unsuspecting prey. They stalk, hunt, shadow, and track their prey, then pounce on them when they least expected. That's not me. I let you know where I'm coming from the get-go.

NINETY-TWO: You can try to justify it any way you want. But, what you did to Bernie yesterday and what you're doing to Rey today is predatory if you ask me.

REY: It's okay.

NINETY-TWO: It's not okay. I don't think people should go around treating others like that. We got to look out for one another. I was trying to give you guys a chance to exhibit your better selves.

CASH: Exhibit our better selves? I like that.

NINETY-TWO: That's right! John, in that bible it says to love thy neighbor as yourself.

JOHN: Not in this bible? Page missing.

CASH: John, they're getting all Kumbaya! Why don't we all hold hands? Ninety-Two, let me ask you something. When has "loving your neighbor" kept mankind from killing his "neighbor," fucking his wife, and eating his children? Ah? I don't think we have to look too far back to find examples of how much we love our neighbors. Let me see. Let's take a look at the last century. Of the top of my head, I can name, let me see, the Armenian genocide. King Leopold genocide of the Congo. The vultures were so fat they couldn't fly. Fifteen million Chinese killed by their good neighbors, the Japanese? They had head-chopping contests. Very neighborly of them. Eighteen million Ukrainians starved to death by that great neighbor Stalin. And, as an act of goodwill toward his neighbors, Hitler and the Nazis killed six million Jews, a million and a half Romani and three million Poles and a bunch of others. And, how about the seventy million killed by Mao? The goodness of man killed something like eighteen million Native Americans in this country alone, and in the Americas, something like one hundred million. Right, Jerome? All the Native People's in the world are under constant threat of annihilation. Then there was Cambodia and Rwanda. And, what about all those other genocides no one talks about anymore? Like Indonesia. The genocide of Algerians. The English starving two million Indians. The Herero. The Irish Potato famine. Yes, that was a genocide, too. The Assyrians. The Greeks. The Haitian by Trujillo. East Timor. The Tasmanians! Tired yet? Because I'm only halfway through. And, I'm not even talking about wars. Let's not forget. We dropped the bomb. Twice! That was very neighborly of us, right? Mankind surely knows how to love his neighbor. Oh yeah, how about the Transatlantic Slave Trade. Conservative estimate—two million dead. The Atlantic Ocean is a cemetery full of my people. It's hallowed ground. That's why I don't swim at the beach. It's like swimming in a watery cemetery of my ancestors.

NINETY-TWO: I agree with you. Man has committed way too many atrocities. The world has gone meshuga, I know. But that's not what humanity is about.

CASH: That's precisely what humanity is about. Sometimes, we participate with indifference. As we speak, the Congo is going through another genocide. Six million Congolese have been murdered since 1996. As many as the Holocaust! But people are too busy sipping their Tazo Green Tea Crème Frappuccino to worry about the people next door. Crimes against humanity seem to be humanity's favorite pastime.

NINETY-TWO: Cash, you talk a good game but let me ask you something—what are you doing about it?

CASH: Me?... Nothing... Like everybody else, like you... Just watching the numbers go up as if I'm watching the stock market ticker tape. Sipping on my Tazo Green Tea Crème Frappuccino... Feeling a little superior to those... afflicted. Hey, Jerome, you're mighty quiet over there. Do you know the total number of native children found buried in Indian boarding schools? Amazingly, the newspapers are finally reporting on it.

JEROME: Why are you going to bring that up? You might offend the sensibility of some good-natured person strolling in the park to commune with nature. They don't want to hear such nonsense… We call those kidnapped children prisoners of war. The schools had that great motto: Kill the Indian, Save the man. What they really did was steal the spirits from those innocent children. Unfortunately, my father attended one of those schools. He called the headmasters Átahsaia, who was a giant cannibalistic demon and an inveterate liar in Zuni folklore. My father used to say that the boarding school killed half of him, making him half dead. He compared himself to a woman who carries a stillborn child inside her womb to term. The difference was my father carried his stillborn child his whole life.

CASH: The guy who championed those boarding schools, I refuse to say his name out loud, said, and I'm paraphrasing: "If millions of Black savages can become so transformed and assimilated, then we can relieve the Indian from their savagery." Man, that guy really loved his neighbors. Hey, John, what does your God have to say about all of this?

JOHN: My God? My God sitting up there in heaven looking at us, saying, "What fuck happen to my Garden of Eden? I give to you food to eat. Water to drink. Fresh air. I could burn your asses in Mercury. Freeze your asses in Pluto, but I make perfect world for you, and you fuck it up." That is what my God saying.

JEROME: When you're up high in a tall skyscraper, and you look down, people become dots. Dots! The Great Spirit looks at us vertically. To Him, there's no difference between one dot and another. The problem with human beings is that we live in a horizontal plane. When we look at one another and all we see is our differences.

CASH: Actually, the first genocide occurred when the Homo Sapiens killed off the Neanderthals. Well, they didn't kill them all. Look at Russian John. He got one Neanderthal-looking mug.

JOHN: (*Embarrassed.*) Fuck you, Cash.

CASH: They did find Neanderthal remains in Belarus. So, you might be related.

JOHN: Like I said. Fuck you! Mahat! Let me tell you how it is. People are Pawns. You can kill Pawns 'cause Pawns nobody give two shits about. Understand? Poor people in Belarus, Pawns. Starve to death in farm. Stupid shit. Living in farm but can't eat. If you had red cheeks, military come, bang, bullet to head. Want to live, don't be Pawn. In chess, Pawns sacrificed like nothing. People give them away. Who cares? It's just a Pawn.

CASH: I don't know about that, John. Pawns aren't worthless. François Phillidor knew that way back in the 1700s when he wrote, "les pions sont l'âme des échecs." Do I have to translate? "Pawns are the soul of chess."

JOHN: Nobody give two shits about soul, too. Only God.

NINETY-TWO: The way I see it, human beings commit cold-blooded murder when their humanity switch has been turned off.

CASH: They never had the switch turned on in the first place. We are born with the humanity switch turned off, and we must turn it on ourselves. That's the reason why it is so easy for people to participate in genocidal policies. You know what's scary? Some people don't even have a switch to turn on.

JOHN: Cash, you know too much about this shit. No good for brain.

CASH: I was doing my dissertation on man's cruelty toward man. But, I focused on that elusive part of man that was essentially good, and I was trying to prove that that good would lead him to his survival despite himself.

NINETY-TWO: What was your conclusion?

CASH: Never got to finish it.

JOHN: Now I know why you drop out. Depressing shit!

CASH: Ninety-Two, don't get me wrong. I respect your point of view being that you're a survivor-

NINETY-TWO: Why are you telling the whole park my business?

CASH: Everyone knows you're a survivor.

NINETY-TWO: Rey didn't!

CASH: My bad. I didn't know it was a secret. I apologize.

NINETY-TWO: Bah. Too late now. The genie is out of the bottle.

REY: You're a survivor? The Holocaust, right? I'm a survivor too. Guatemalan genocide. One of the genocides no one talks about. They called it the "Silent Holocaust."

NINETY-TWO: I know. Horrific. Just horrific.

REY: The only survivor I know is my uncle, but he never wants to talk about it.

NINETY-TWO: Not the best club to be a member of. No application necessary. As a matter of fact, someone else must make you a member against your will.

REY: How did you survive?

NINETY-TWO: Survived? If you can call it that! But, to answer your question—Chess.

REY: Chess? If it saved your life, why don't you play anymore?

NINETY-TWO: For that very same reason.

REY: I don't understand.

NINETY-TWO: I'm just keeping a promise. Listen, go home before it's too late.

REY: I lost Stuart's money.

NINETY-TWO: Give me your phone number, and I'll pass it to Stuart when he comes around. He'll understand. It isn't the first time something like this happened here.

REY: (*Rey hands a business card to Ninety-Two.*) I actually thought I was going to beat them and get my uncle's money back. I mean, I'm not in great form. But, I'm not as bad as they made me seem. I thought I had a chance.

JEROME: A lot of people come here thinking like that, and leave poorer than when they came in.

NINETY-TWO: Playing chess is a muscle, a reflex for these guys. It's all they do, day in day out.

REY: If I were in better shape, I...

NINETY-TWO: You're off form. It's understandable.

REY: Fuck! Not only did I lose Stuart's money, but I also lost part of my rent. My girl said she'd leave me if I did something like this again.

NINETY-TWO: I'm sure she'll forgive you.

REY: I don't think so. Not this time. I've been on a short leash since I returned from...

NINETY-TWO: Women will surprise you.

REY: I can't go home like this… It isn't about the money! *(Rey walks up to John's table as he rolls up his sleeves.)*

NINETY-TWO: Kid! Kid!

> *Rey's phone rings. He looks at it and puts it back in his pocket.*

NINETY-TWO: That kid reminds me of myself when I was his age. And that's not a good thing.

JEROME: He has the same look my father had before he walked into the desert never to be heard from again.

> *At John's table.*

REY: Fuck it! For all the marbles!

> *Rey places the rest of his money on the table and sits. Cash and John grin from ear to ear. As the lights fade, they make a series of moves. The loud ticking of a clock is heard.*

CHESS GAME #6
"Perpetual"
[White - Rey] [Black - Cash]

1.e2-e4 e7-e6 2.f2-f4 d7-d5 3.e4-e5 c7-c5 4.Ng1-f3 Nb8-c6 5.Bf1-b5 a7-a6 6.Bb5xc6+ b7xc6 7.d2-d3 d5-d4 8.O-O Ng8-e7 9.Nb- d2 Ne7-d5 10.Nd2-e4 Bf8-e7 11.Bc1-d2 f7-f5

END OF ACT 1

ACT 2

> In the darkness, a clock is heard ticking along with chess pieces being slammed on the chess table. Lights rise. Cash and Rey rattle off a bunch of quick moves. This is the continuation of the last game in act one. Rey starts to think before making a move.
>
> We are now in the end game. Many pieces have been exchanged. The positions of the pieces are as follows:
>
> For the White Pieces, the King is on h2. Rook on c5. Pawn on h3. Pawn on b4.
>
> For the Black Pieces, the King is on d4. Bishop on e2. Pawn on d3. Pawn on c6.

CHESS GAME #6
"Perpetual"
[White - Rey] [Black - Cash]

47.Rc5xc6 Kd4-e3 48.b4-b5 d3-d2.
49.Rc6-e6+ Ke3-f2. 50.Re6-d6 Kf2-Ke3 51.b5-b6 Be2-d3 52.Rd6-e6+ Ke3-f2

> *Jerome's table.*

NINETY-TWO: He's a survivor, Jerome.

JEROME: I know, I heard.

NINETY-TWO: How do you reconcile that you are alive when your love ones didn't make it?

How do you pick up the pieces when there's no book with instructions? No manual...

JEROME: I know.

> *At John's table. Cash and Rey play as John talks on a cell phone.*

JOHN: Yury... It's me, John. Chess player John... Yeah, broken hand, Johnny... Not funny, Yury. Not funny... I got your money... Yeah, not playing with foot, ha, ha... Two hundred buckaroos on the fifth race in Aqueduct on Salvation. Got to go. Got another call. Hey, Charisse... Me, John... Right here. Cash. Charisse.

CASH: Give me my phone... I have the money for the bike. Happy? I'll deliver it in the morning. Look, I'm in the middle of a game, and I don't want to be rude, but I have to go... Charisse, please don't start... Like I said, I'll deliver the bike in the morning. Goodbye Charisse... Goodbye... Bye! (*Cash ends call. Imitating Charisse.*) Are you still wasting your life? When are you going to grow up? You're so smart. You could've been a professor. Why are you wasting your talent hustling in the street? What kind of example are you setting for your son? (*Stops imitating Charisse.*) That's why I don't answer the phone when she calls. But you had to go and answer it.

JOHN: My bad. Forget her. Breathe. Breathe motherfucker. Breathe.

CASH: I'm good. I'm good. Hey, Ninety-Two, are you ready for our daily challenge?

JEROME: Don't answer him.

CASH: Don't tell me you're scared.

NINETY-TWO: Let me at him.

JEROME: You can't let him disrespect you and then joke with him.

CASH: Are you ready, Ninety-Two?

NINETY-TWO: Bring it, schmendrik.

CASH: Today you will go down! I have three brand new chess quotes for you. Guess who said this one. "Chess-like love, like music, has the power to make men happy."

NINETY-TWO: You got to come with one harder than that, you schmuck. The chess theoretician, Siegbert Tarrasch!

CASH: Okay, Okay! Try this one on for size. Chess is everything: art, science, and sport.

NINETY-TWO: That one is easy too, you putz. Former World Champion Anatoly Karpov.

CASH: Okay, okay. I have one more! And this one will stump you.

NINETY-TWO: Dream on.

CASH: Care to put a small wager on it?

NINETY-TWO: You should know by now, I don't gamble.

CASH: All men gamble. When you buy a sandwich at a deli, you're gambling that the deli man might not have washed his hands after he took a dump. When you cross the street, you are taking a chance that the brakes on the approaching car might or might not work. You have money in the stock market. That's gambling.

NINETY-TWO: I don't gamble on games. How about that?

CASH: Fair enough. Fair enough. But you are taking the fun out of it. Here's your final quote of the day. "For me, chess is life, and every game is like a new life. Every chess player gets to live many lives in one lifetime."

Ninety-Two hesitates, but he knows the answer.

CASH: I think I finally stumped him.

NINETY-TWO: Give me a minute.

CASH: I thought I'd never get to see this day. Your time is running out, Ninety-Two.

NINETY-TWO: Grandmaster, Eduard Gufeld. And, let me add that truer words have never been spoken. Hah!

CASH: Man, I almost had you.

NINETY-TWO: Bupkus! (*Enjoys his victory.*)

CASH: I'll stump you one day.

NINETY-TWO: Keep dreaming.

> Move played
> Rey [W] - 53. b6-b7

REY: I got one! Who said, "The profuse phallic symbolism of chess provides some fantasy of the homosexual wish, particularly the desire for mutual masturbation?"

> *Everyone stares at Rey like, "What the fuck did he just say?"*

REY: I didn't make it up. Just quoting it.

NINETY-TWO: American Grandmaster and psychologist, Ruben Fine. That's who said it.

CASH: Mutual masturbation! Suppose that every chess game is the equivalent to masturbation. In that case, one can only surmise that chess players must really be devoted to masturbating.

NINETY-TWO: Isn't everybody?

CASH: Ninety-Two, you old dog, don't tell me you're still? (*Mimes masturbating.*)

NINETY-TWO: It's good for arthritis. Hand dexterity. You should try it sometime.

CASH: No, no. I'm a master beater, not a masturbator, mister.

> Move played:
> Cash [B] – 53. d2-d1=Queen

NINETY-TWO: You don't know what you're missing.

CASH: See, see what that little blue pill has done?

JOHN: Cash, pay attention to game. What going on here?

NINETY-TWO: If Rey queens his Pawn, he'll get mated on g1.

JOHN: Shut the fuck up!

CASH: Ninety-Two, move away from the table.

> Move played:
> Rey [W] - 54. Re6-f6+

REY: Check!

CASH: Got to respect a check.

> Cash [B] - 54. Kf2-e2

JOHN: Always respect check!

> Rey [W] - 55. Rf6-e6+

REY: Check.

CASH: Check must be respected!

> Moves played.
> Cash [B] – 55. Ke2-f2
> Rey [W] – 56. Re6-f6+

REY: Check!

CASH: Perpetual check. You can't win. Draw!

> *Rey thinks for a short moment.*

CASH: You can't win unless I move my King to the wrong square. Draw?

REY: I guess. Okay. Draw. Man, I thought I had you. I was up the exchange.

CASH: Man, material doesn't mean anything. It's about the energy field the pieces create when they cooperate with each other. You could be up a Queen and get mated by a Pawn.

> *They set up the pieces on the board. Cash is very upset.*

NINETY-TWO: Close but no cigar!

CASH: Rey, are you ready for the next one?

REY: Of course. I'm getting closer.

CASH: Double the bet. Four hundred?

REY: Sure. I should've won the last game.

CASH: Hold on a second. Ninety-Two, come over here. I got a bone to pick with you.

NINETY-TWO: (*Jokingly to Jerome.*) I think I'm in trouble. (*Ninety-Two walks over to John's table.*)

CASH: What the hell are you doing calling out moves during the game?

NINETY-TWO: (*Dismissive.*) You're taking his money anyway.

JOHN: Don't call out move in man's game. Understand?

CASH: You crossed a line, Ninety-Two. We have just one rule in the park. Just one rule! That rule is, in case you've forgotten, that no one gives moves to a player during a game.

JOHN: Eleventh commandment: Thou shall not call out move. Understand?

NINETY-TWO: You want me to apologize? I apologize. There! Can I go back to my friend?

CASH: You're not getting off that easily. Calling out moves is taboo for a reason. This sacred rule was created so that the denizens in this park could maintain a semblance of civility. Violating this rule brings about a state of anomie, chaos, disorder, pandemonium, and bedlam. And, we've all experienced that in the past. Because of that rule, we've had many years of peacetime in this park. As they say, it has kept the barbarians at the gate. You violated that sacred rule, Ninety-Two, and you know better than that. By opening your mouth and putting my money at risk, you have imperiled the peace we all cherish so much.

JEROME: Are you going to keep talking? What, you have diarrhea of the mouth? The man apologized.

CASH: Jerome, as tenuous as our relationship is, you and I have never had to have this conversation.

JEROME: I remember there was another rule that has been abandoned... one shall not steal another's player.

CASH: Are you still upset we took Rey away from you? Look, we were reeling him in when you snatched him away. Besides, that rule was made for money players. And you're not a money player.

NINETY-TWO: Oy. He just won't stop with the spiel. Okay, I won't do it again. Happy?

CASH: I'm not finished with you. You're the one who opened Pandora's box. See, I'm not forcing Rey to play, nor did I hypnotize him. And, I'm not keeping him here against his will. Am I Rey?

REY: No.

CASH: There you have it.

NINETY-TWO: Are you going to keep going? My God! So much shmegegge over nothing.

CASH: It ain't nonsense Ninety-Two. I got my Yiddish down, too. Remember, I'm a polyglot. You don't understand the severity of your actions. Maybe, John is right. You both should go to Central Park. This isn't the park of yesteryear. Leave this place to us.

CHESS GAME #7
"Didn't See It"
[White - Cash] [Black- Rey]

1.e2-e4 e7-e6 2.d2-d4 d7-d5 3.Nb1-c3 d5xe4 4.Nc3-e4 Nb8-d7 5.Ng1-f3 Ng8-f6 6.Nf3-g5 Bf8-e7 7.Ng5xf7 Ke8xf7 8.Ne4-g5+ Kf7-g8 9.Ng5xe6 Qd8-e8 10.Ne6-c7 Be7-b4 Mate

> *Cash starts the clock and makes a move, then a flurry of moves gets played.*

NINETY-TWO: You would like that, wouldn't you? (*To Jerome.*) The chutzpah on this guy!

CASH: John, they think they're walking around with halos on their heads. And I know for a fact they're not.

JEROME: What the hell are you talking about?

NINETY-TWO: Bah, he's just shooting off his mouth.

CASH: Let's start with you, Jerome. Didn't you sell your boat when it became more difficult to make a living fishing?

JEROME: Yeah, so?

CASH: So, you sort of passed the buck. Someone else was left holding the bag. Well, in your case, a boat.

JEROME: That's bullshit. I made it clear to the buyer that you had to go out further and further out into the ocean to catch enough fish to make it worthwhile. And I was getting too old to be out on the sea for days at a time.

CASH: I remember the day when the "buyer" came to the park in tears, willing to sell it back for half of what he paid.

JEROME: A year later! I had already settled into my new life. Go to hell.

CASH: Touchy! Now, it's your turn Ninety-Two. You are one sneaky feller.

NINETY-TWO: Don't know what you're referring to.

CASH: After the market crashed a few years ago, your son, Jeff, came around looking for you. He was so - how can I say it? Euphoric, I think that's the right word—that you had advised him and the family to sell off their stocks right before the market crashed. Somehow you had access to insider information. And I started asking myself, how did Ninety-Two, a simple "barber," have this information? Then, I thought about your clientele. Wall Street types. And I concluded that someone had to have given you a tip that the shit was about to hit the fan. Which is illegal, by the way. And that's how you were able to save your family's finances.

NINETY-TWO: And what's wrong with that?

CASH: Nothing. But one thing concerns me. You didn't let anyone else know. Dr. Lee lost a large portion of his investments. Stuart got hit pretty hard, too. And we consider those two our associates—almost friends. We lost a lot of fish because of the Financial Crash.

NINETY-TWO: What do you want me to say? That I care about my family, and I would do whatever I needed to do to help them out? Guilty!
I wasn't going to let them get destroyed.

CASH: I understand. You were looking out for yourself and your loved ones. That's the way it's supposed to be. Look, our system is predicated on hustling. The strong hustle the weak. The smart hustle the dumb. The informed hustle the uninformed. And on and on. I didn't make the rules, I just abide by them. I'm so proud of you both. You hustled the system. You see, we're not that different.

JEROME: Don't ever compare yourself to us. Not even in your dreams.

CASH: Oh, Jerome, Jerome, Jerome!

>Move played:
>Rey [B] - 10. Be7-b4+

REY: Check!

JOHN: (*To Rey.*) That's checkmate. You idiot for life!

CASH: How could I miss that?

REY: Checkmate? How?

NINETY-TWO: You're checking him with two pieces at the same time. The Bishop and the Queen. Discovered double check! The most lethal move on the chess. (*Points it out on the chessboard.*) See? He has nowhere to move his King. Congratulations! You won!

JOHN: Lucky asshole. Didn't know it was mate.

REY: I won! I don't believe it. What a relief! Unbelievable! If I would've lost, I wouldn't have been able to go home. My girl would've killed me.

NINETY-TWO: (*To Jerome.*) Did you see that?

JEROME: He got lucky!

REY: You guys need to pay up.

JOHN: Fuck Cash. How could you lose to this patzer? I know why. Fucking Ninety-Two.

NINETY-TWO: Hey, hey, Rey beat him fair and square.

JOHN: But you talking all this shit to him. And Cash, you shut fuck up, too, and play!

CASH: Everyone needs to zip it!

REY: You guys haven't paid me yet.

> *John and Cash throw their money on the table.*

CASH: Are you ready now?

REY: I don't know.

CASH: Here we go again with this tired song and dance.

REY: No, I mean, maybe I should take my losses and go home. At least, I got some of my money back.

CASH: You beat me once, maybe you'll do it again.

REY: (*Pause.*) That's a good point. You've convinced me. Okay, let's play another. See what happens.

JEROME: Rey, don't let it go to your head. Hustlers usually throw games near the end of a match to give the fish a false sense of confidence, so they'll continue playing.

CASH: Why are giving away the secrets of our profession?

JEROME: I think the man should be able to make an informed decision.

CASH: Like the guy who bought your boat!

JOHN: Jeromes, give rectal examination to yourself or go see Dr. Lee. Come on, Cash, flim flam him. Then rope ah dope him. Then trick him and dick 'em. Slice him and dice him. And to put him out of misery, duke 'em and nuke 'em! Then stab him in the neck!

CASH: Same bet?

REY: Okay, sure.

CHESS GAME #8
"Who Da Man?"
[White - Rey] [Black - Cash]

1. e2-e4 c7-c6 2. Nb1-c3 d7-d5 3.Ng1-f3 d5xe4 4. Nc3xe4 Bc8-f5 5. Ne4-g3 Bf5-g6 6. h2-h4 h7-h6 7. Nf3-e5 Bg6-h7 8. Qd1-h5 g7-g6 9. Bf1- c4 e7-e6 10. Qh5-d2 Ng8-f6 11. Ne5xf7 Ke8xf7 12. Qe2xe6 Kf7-g7 13. Qe6-f7#

> *Rey starts the clock. A bunch of moves are played.*

JOHN: Man, concentrate. Stop pussyfooting. Beat the hell out this sinner. Put that beef stroganoff in him.

CASH: Oh, no, no, no, no. You can't make a move like that on me. Now, you must be punished. Who's the man?

JOHN: You da man!

CASH: I said, who's the man?

JOHN: You da man!

Move played:
Cash [B] – 5. Bc8-f5

CASH: Oh, yeah, I'm sticking this Bishop deep into your position, Rey, baby! No Vaseline, baby. He's going to need a proctologist. Where's Dr. Lee when you need him. Somebody please call an ambulance! Because this man needs to have this beef stroganoff extracted from deep within. I said, who's the man?

They play a few more moves.

JOHN: You da man!

CASH: Rey, who's the man?

JOHN: Who da man, Rey?

CASH: Answer me. Ah, Rey? Who's the man? You should resign, Rey. Why are you still playing this game?

JOHN: Come, Rey, start new game, don't embarrass yourself!

CASH: Quit, Rey. Time is money, and money is time! If you misuse it, it's a crime! Who's the man?

JOHN: You da man!

CASH: Can't hear you.

JOHN: You da man!

CASH: I said, who's the man?

> *Suddenly the hustlers get quiet. There's panic in their eyes. Ninety-Two sensing something wrong walks over to the table and studies the board. Rey leans back, having a silent conversation with himself, then comes to a decision.*

> Move played:
> Rey [W] - 11. Ne5xf7

REY: I'm the man! Who's the man? I'm the man! Who's the man?

NINETY-TWO: You're the man!

JOHN: You fucked up, Cash. How could you leave King open like that?

CASH: I didn't see it.

> Move played:
> Cash [B] – 10. Ke8xf7

REY: Right about now, you're beginning to hate your game. Am I right?

CASH: You don't have enough time on the clock to beat me.

JOHN: Yeah, Rey, your time running out.

REY: I got more time than I know what to do with.

> Move played:

Rey [W] - 11. Qe2-e6+

REY: Check! Make your move.

CASH: Damn!

> *Cash makes his move. Rey picks up a chess piece slamming it down.*

> Moves played:
> Cash [B] – 11. Kf7-g7
> Rey [W] – 12. Qe6-f7#

REY: Mate! Pay the man!

JOHN: Shit, man! How you lose that game?

CASH: I blundered, that's all.

JOHN: Jesus H. Christ! I don't believe this shit.

> *Cash and John throw their money on the table. Rey has a confident look. Cash now looks insecure.*

NINETY-TWO: Kid, just get up and leave. Luck has a way of running out.

JEROME: He's right, Rey.

REY: I can't quit now when I'm on a winning streak.

JOHN: Cash, what fuck going on? You spotting to him too much time. Big handicap.

CASH: Wait! Wait! A few minutes ago, I was mating this guy in the opening, and now he beats me two games in a row. I think we're being hustled!

REY: I was just lucky. (*Broad smile.*)

CASH: You've been hustling us from the moment you walked into this park! You were throwing all those games you lost! Weren't you?

REY: Okay, you got me. Guilty as charged! I heard you guys were the best, and to hustle the best, you need to execute a good game plan. Had to catch you off guard. Make you overconfident.

CASH: I'm quite aware of the overconfidence effect theory.

REY: Theory or not, I caught you with your pants down.

NINETY-TWO: Very clever.

CASH: Very predatory of him, right Ninety-Two?

NINETY-TWO: Should've let me interfere. Cash, you and John misread the situation because of the desperate state of your finances. On another day, you would've spotted his intentions the moment he walked into the park.

CASH: (*Sarcastically.*) Great insight, Ninety-Two.

REY: Are you guys ready for the next one? I'm just getting warmed up.

JOHN: No more chess for me.

REY: (*Laughs.*) I didn't know I was playing with a bunch of quitters.

CASH: I don't run from anyone. I've beaten stronger players than you. And John, you can't quit. Besides, I was giving you huge time odds. Let's see how you do with even time. My five minutes against your five minutes!

REY: Let's get it on then!

JOHN: You better win! Remember my hand. Do it for my hand!

CHESS GAME #9
"River Of Blood"
[White -Rey] [Black-Rey]

1.f2-f4 d7-d5 2.Ng1-f3 Nb8-c6 3.e2-e3
Bc8-g4 4.b2-b3 e7-e5 5.f4xe5 Nc6xe5 6.Bf1-e2
Bg4xf3 7.Be2xf3 Ng8-f6 8.Bc1-b2 Bf8-d6 9.O-O
Nf6-e4 10.Nb1-c3 Qd8-h4 11.Nc3-d5 Qh4xh2+
12.Kg1xh2 Ne5-f3+ 13.Kh2-h3 Ne-g5+ 14.Kh3-g4 h7-h5+ 15.Kg4-f5 g7-g6 16. Kf4-f6 Ke7-f8

> *Rey starts Cash's clock. They make a few moves.*

REY: You ever heard about the Popol Vuh?

JOHN: What fuck guy talking about?

CASH: Of course! The Mayan book of the Dawn of Man. What about it?

REY: According to the Popol Vuh, these Fish Men, half men - half fish, came down to earth from the sky to destroy the wicked, those who preyed on the weak and those who dealt in the misery of others. You can say I'm a Fish Man. I came down to set the park straight. You guys took advantage of Bernie. And anybody that fucks with Bernie has to deal with me. He can't defend himself. But, that's what I'm here for. Payback time!

CASH: So, now we're wicked. And, you're going to exact your revenge on us?

REY: People underestimate the power of revenge.

JOHN: Vengeance mine, said the lord. Don't mess with God. He get your ass.

REY: John, are you talking about the God who just sat underneath the shade of a tree twiddling his thumbs as all these atrocious acts against humanity were being committed? The so-called God, who drowned the world once and has promised to destroy it again? That God? The one that seems more like a homicidal maniac than a loving old man with magical powers. That God? I'll take the Fish Men over God anytime.

JOHN: God, I don't know him. I'm moving away from you just in case he strike you down.

REY: *(To Cash.)* You're not winning another game. You got to pay for what you did to Bernie. I owe him everything. If he hadn't taken me fishing on the day my village was massacred, I would've been slaughtered along with everyone else. Like my mother, my little brother, and fifteen family members—hacked to death by machetes. I think it's time to sacrifice my Queen! Watch this killer move. CHECK!

> Move played:
> Rey [B] - 11. Qh4xh2

REY: I think, no, I know you're in trouble. Your King is going on a long march through the line of fire. He better duck.

JOHN: He got nothing!

> Moves played:
> Cash [W] - 12. Kg1xh2
> Rey [B] - 12. Ne5-f3+

REY: CHECK! King hunt! That King better get on his tricycle. You can run, but you cannot hide.

JOHN: Come on, Cash!

> Moves played:
> Cash [W] - 13. Kh2-h3.
> Rey [B] - 13. Ne4-g5+

REY: CHECK! This King hunt reminds me of when the army picked up our tracks in the woods. We heard the dogs coming from all directions. Do you hear the dogs barking, Cash? Do you hear the engines of the army trucks? Do you hear the sound of machine guns fired into the air? Do you hear the shouting of the soldiers? How long would you be able to hold your breath underwater in a river of blood if your life depended on it? Where is that King going now?

>Moves played:
>Cash [W] - 14. Kh3-g4
>Rey [B] - 14. h7-h5+

REY: CHECK! Bernie knew how to get us out. But you, my friend, have no way out! We spent three months in the woods hiding out, moving from place to place. That guy you took advantage of made me a cardboard chessboard. He collected rocks and sticks, making chess pieces out of them because chess was the only thing that kept me calm when the soldiers got so close, we could see their uniforms through the tall grass. He told me that makeshift chessboard had special powers, and it would keep us safe. It never failed us. That's the kind of man he is, and I'll give up my life for him.

>Moves played:
>Cash [W] - 15. Kg4-f5
>Rey [B] - 15. g7-g6+

REY: CHECK! I said, CHECK!

>Move played:
>Cash [W] - 16. Kf4-f6

REY: And after all those checks, now I play a quiet move. SH!

> Move played:
> Rey [B.] - 16. Ke7-f8

REY: Are you going to resign, or are you going to make me mate you? What is it going to be?

CASH: Draw?

REY: (*Laughs at him.*) You want a draw? Please, someone, get this man a box of crayons so he could draw a picture of this beautiful checkmate! Don't embarrass yourself. Resign! A toast! To the goodness of man and to good neighbors!

CASH: You got it! I resign.

JOHN: I don't believe this shit. I don't believe it. I don't believe it.

> *The hustlers throw their money on the table with disgust. Cash walks to the water fountain, followed by John. They are furious.*

JOHN: Cash, what the fuck?

CASH: Not now, John.

JOHN: Yes, now! Yes, now.

CASH: Look, I'm in no mood.

JOHN: I'm in no mood, too.

CASH: Like I said, stay away from me.

JOHN: You said you could beat him.

CASH: That's what I'm trying to do!

JOHN: That's your problem. Trying. Do. Do. You play scare.

CASH: Do you want to play him? Ah? Didn't think so, because he'd wipe the floor with you. Now, can I please drink my water in peace?

REY: Be careful, there might be an alligator waiting for you to take a sip of water.

NINETY-TWO: Rey, you should go home.

REY: Nah, I want all their money. People got to pay for what they do to others. There have to be consequences. They can't be getting away with it.

NINETY-TWO: You can win, but in winning, you can end up the ultimate loser.

REY: What the hell are you talking about?

NINETY-TWO: Do you realize you're losing control? You're right there on that precipice. You're like a ticking time bomb about to go off.

REY: I'm just doling out justice like the Fish Men. You don't know what you're talking about.

NINETY-TWO: (*Ninety-Two puts sleeve to his nose, taking a deep breath.*) You hear this man, Jerome? I don't know what I'm talking about. I know well what it is to lose control. You asked me earlier why I didn't play chess... I don't like to talk about it, but I'm going to make an exception for you because you're standing on that ledge, my friend. The reason I don't play chess anymore and haven't for over sixty years it's because I wagered my father's and sister's lives in the last game I ever played.

REY: And you lost!

NINETY-TWO: Nah... I won... I won. But there's this little-known concept called the defeat of victory. You lose, although you win. The Commandant of the concentration camp heard about this kid, who was a chess prodigy. This kid had the distinguished position at the camp of shaving women's heads before they were led into the gas chambers... Me... me. One day he brought me to his beautiful home, right there at edge of the camp, and challenged me to a game. Before we played, I asked to put a wager on the game. If I won, my father and sister would be released. He was very confident he was going to beat this emaciated kid, so he agreed. I wasn't going to lose that game. I couldn't lose that game. I must admit I was physically weak, but chess-wise I was in pretty good form. See, every night under the cover of darkness we, the prisoners, played chess in the barracks without a chessboard. You hear people yelling out moves. Knight captures f6. Rook d8 check. King h7. Checkmate... I was weak. So I raised the sleeve of my shirt to my nose and breathed in the ashes of all those poor souls who had perished. (*He puts sleeve to nose, taking deep breath.*) The spirits, to whom those ashes

135

belonged, supplied me with the strength I needed. After an eternally long game, I finally beat him. It was a small victory in the scope of things... Tiny. Still, I felt a significant one, even though it was only a measly chess game. After the game, he drove me to a riverbank and released me. I was so excited because I expected to see my father and sister waiting for me there. And I just wanted to run into their arms for an eternity. You know... and... we could start putting this nightmare behind us. The commander was about to drive off, and he must've seen the confusion in my face because he stopped the car, and said matter of factly, that my father and sister had been put to death while we played the chess game... That day I made a promise to myself never to play this game again.

JEROME: Are you okay?

NINETY-TWO: Yes, Jerome. Thank you for asking. Rey, I know every wrinkle on that precipice. Every single one. Don't know how many people I beat to a pulp. Maybe, what we're looking for is for someone to take mercy on us and put us out of our misery. And, you are right there on the brink. Am I wrong? Am I?

> *Rey walks away from Ninety-Two and over to the hustlers.*

NINETY-TWO: Don't walk away from me. (*To Jerome.*) That kid! I've been where he's headed. And, it ain't a pretty place. A bad end! A bad end!

REY: (*Rey reads a text message.*) You guys ready?

JOHN: Get out my face, man!

CASH: That's it for me!

REY: What do you mean? My work isn't finished here. You can't quit.

CASH: You took our money. You've hustled us. You've won. There's nothing else to prove. We only got a few loose bills and chump change left.

REY: You're wrong! This isn't over. You left Bernie with nothing. So, get out those loose bills!

CASH: I see this isn't just a hustle for you. You want to hurt us. Like those half men-half fish.

REY: That's right. So, get your money out and put it on the table.

CASH: Nuh, nuh! I don't think so my brother. You're making this more than just a chess game. I'm not participating in your little revenge plot. I read about people like you in Psychology 101.

JOHN: (*John laughs.*) Damn Psychology 101. Not even advance shit. 101!

CASH: You know, you and Bernie are so much alike. It's all or nothing with you guys. Case in point—you just won, but you can't walk away. I don't know what that is. Bernie could've gotten up many times but didn't. Like something was keeping him here. As if he wanted to be punished.

REY: (*Self-conscious.*) I'll give you odds. What do you want?

CASH: See? You keep proving my point. Look, I don't want anything. We're not playing. Come on, John.

> *Cash and John walk to John's table. Rey reads a text message.*

JOHN: Maybe, we should listen to offer. See what he going to give.

CASH: Follow my lead.

JOHN: I just want my money back.

CASH: Sh! Don't kill the hustle! There he comes!

REY: Did you guys talk it over? What are the odds going to be?

CASH: Didn't I tell you we weren't playing?

JOHN: No playing! Over! Over!

REY: I'll give you time odds. I'll give you five minutes and I'll take three!

CASH: I said no. We're not playing.

REY: Are you kidding me? You're not taking five to three? (*To Ninety-Two.*) You believe this?

NINETY-TWO: You should be happy. I've never seen anyone take their money like you have.

REY: Jerome, you've ever seen some chicken shit like this before?

JEROME: You shouldn't be talking to me right now. I'm not very happy being used in your little scheme.

REY: I'm sorry about that, but it was necessary to bring their guards down.

JEROME: I don't appreciate it.

REY: Maybe, I'll play you after I finish them off.

JEROME: Don't do me any favors.

REY: (*To Cash and John.*) Okay, fish! What is it going to be?

JOHN: Fish? I no fish!

CASH: (*To John.*) Keep your skirt on! (*To Rey.*) Didn't I make myself abundantly clear? I thought I made myself clear.

REY: Very clear! Very, very clear.

CASH: Come on John, let's play a game.

Cash and John start playing.

Moves played:
John [W] - 1. e2-e4

Cash [B] - 1. e7-e5
John [W] - 2. Ng1-f3
Cash [B] - 2. Nb8-c6
John [W] - 3. Bf1-b5
Cash [B] - 3. a7-a6

REY: I can see why you quit school. Things get tough, you quit. Once a quitter, always a quitter!

CASH: It's better not to talk about things you don't know anything about.

JOHN: Don't listen to him. He's trying to get in your head. (*To Rey.*) Hey, shit face! Stop talking shit and swallow it.

REY: Cash is sensitive. What some professor didn't like you? They threw your ass out. What happened? You failed? I hate fucking quitters! When Bernie and I were being hunted, he broke his ankle, and he didn't give up. And look at you.

CASH: If you want to get in my head, you must come with more than that.

REY: Okay. Bernie told me you kept him hostage here. That the two of you wouldn't let him leave until he paid you.

JOHN: Mister, no hostage here.

CASH: It didn't go down like that.

REY: Who am I going to believe, my uncle who saved my life, or two hustlers?

CASH: I was going to go with him to his apartment to pick up the money.

REY: Bullshit!

CASH: Ask anyone!

NINETY-TWO: It's true.

JEROME: They're telling the truth.

REY: I don't believe any of you. Bernie told me he couldn't leave.

CASH: Maybe, he misunderstood.

REY: Nah, you don't misunderstand something like that!

CASH: You and your uncle seem to suffer from paranoia. I'd check that out if I were you.

REY: Bernie wouldn't make things up. I just want you to know that I'm aware of what you did to him.

CASH: Ninety-Two and even Jerome, who can't stand the sight of us, just told you we didn't keep your uncle here against his will. And yet you choose to believe in this delusion. Believe what you want, then. I'm done with you. (*To John.*) Whose move is it?

JOHN: Mines.

John makes a chess move. Rey paces around John's table. He gets a phone message, looks at it, and puts the phone away.

REY: I tell you what. In addition to time odds, I'll give you money odds.

CASH: Money odds? What exactly are we talking about here?

JOHN: How much?

CASH: You got our attention.

REY: Everything you lost against what you got in your pockets.

JOHN: Sounds good to me.

CASH: Nah, man. If we win, we just come out even. We would've put a whole day's work for nothing.

REY: So, what do you want?

CASH: Everything we got against everything you got. One hundred percent to one hundred percent!

REY: Do I have stupid written on my forehead?

CASH: No. But I think you're a very smart man. Smart enough to know that we won't play if our conditions aren't met.

REY: You know I can walk away having the satisfaction of busting your ass.

CASH: So, walk away then. There are four exits to choose from. Go ahead. Put one foot in front of the other. I don't see you moving. Most men would walk out of the park and brag about how they hustled the hustlers of Washington Square Park. But you can't do that, can you? You want it all. Therefore, you can't take any satisfaction that you've beaten us. And although you won, you haven't humiliated us, and that's what you're really after. Right? So, you haven't been able to exact total revenge on us. But if you want to get your little revenge, you have to take the risk of losing it all. Hey, as long as we have loose change in our pockets, we are the real winners. So, you have a big decision to make. All or nothing!

Rey is lost in his thoughts.

NINETY-TWO: Rey! Rey! Hey Rey! You're not considering those odds, right? Take that money and take your girl and Bernie out to a nice dinner.

REY: How much money do you guys have?

John and Cash throw their money on the table.

CASH: Altogether about nine dollars, more or less. What do you have?

REY: Fifteen hundred more or less.

CASH: Sounds good to me.

NINETY-TWO: A fool's bet. Cash is too good at those odds. Crazy!

CASH: So, what are you going to do?

NINETY-TWO: Don't let them try to talk you into this insane bet.

CASH: Why don't you let the man make up his own mind?

REY: You got change in your pockets? Put it on the table.

> Cash and John throw a few coins on the table.

NINETY-TWO: Kid!

REY: Now, it's even. Let's do it! Are you ready?

CASH: I was born ready.

> Rey and Cash set up the pieces. They look at each other like two boxers who want to cause harm to one another.

NINETY-TWO: Jerome, maybe he'll listen to you. Talk to him.

JEROME: I'm not getting involved.

REY: (*Rey cell phone rings. He looks at it. He stops the clock.*) Fuck! She just won't leave me alone. Got to take it. (*Rey walks to water fountain.*) Yeah?... Yeah, I got all your texts... Why? Why?

Cash and John talk about the game, but we don't hear them.

REY: I told you I was going to beat them, right? I'm taking them for everything they have. You should see their faces, Maritza... Just one more game and I'll be on my way. Tell Bernie there isn't anything to worry about. I got his money back. I'll be home soon... Stop bringing up Guatemala... Yes, I realize what I did. So what? Look, I'm not going home until I finish them off... Why are you asking me? I don't know. In the box, I guess. Ask Bernie, I don't have it... What would I be doing with Bernie's gun, Maritza?... I'm not going home right now... What do you mean my time ran out?... Is that how you want it? Fine! It's over! (*Shuts phone down. Walks back to John's table.*)

NINETY-TWO: Is everything okay?

REY: Yeah, yeah...

NINETY-TWO: Doesn't sound like it.

REY: She's so persistent, you know? Can't let things go.

NINETY-TWO: I hope you don't mind me asking, but what happened in Guatemala? It seems to be a bone of contention between you two.

REY: (*Pause.*) A little over a month ago, I received a letter from the Guatemalan government informing me that they had found my mother's remains in a mass grave. You know, DNA match. So, I went there to give her a proper burial. I thought it was going to be easy. Bury her. Buy her a tombstone, and come back to my everyday life. Maybe, that's what I wanted to believe. I met some of the other victims' relatives there, and they told me who oversaw the massacre of my village. It seemed like everyone knew who he was, including the government, but he was a wealthy landowner and a military officer. He was untouchable. He had gotten away with it. I decided to go see him. I mean, in my wildest dreams, I never thought I'd have the chance to come face to face with the man who's given me the only nightmare I've ever had. I brought a gun with me. I didn't know what I was walking into… This young sweet Mayan maid who reminded me of my mother took me to his parlor. I sat at a table where there was this beautifully hand-carved wooden chessboard. He came in, and the girl got really nervous and left quickly. He sat across from me, and we started playing without saying a word. When I told him my mother's name, he thought for a second, then said she did housework for his family when she was about thirteen. Then, he laughed and said he had made her into a woman. What a great piece of ass she was. He laughed and then asked, "What the fuck you want from me? I heard she had some half-breed bastard. You think I'm your father? Came to claim your piece of the estate? You ain't getting shit from me! Then, told me to get the fuck out of his house before he threw my ass out. I pointed the gun right at his heart. All of a sudden, he changed his tune. Started whimpering. Saying shit like… like… he had grandchildren. And that his daughter was pregnant. He didn't realize that shit made me angrier. He took my family from me, and now he wanted me to let him live for his. Can you believe that shit? I don't remember the gun going off. But there he was lying on the floor in a pool of his own blood.

NINETY-TWO: Did your nightmares stop?

REY: What?

NINETY-TWO: Your nightmares did they stop?

REY: No… But at least I don't feel impotent anymore. (*Rey takes a few steps towards John's table.*)

NINETY-TWO: How did your uncle take it?

REY: My uncle?... He started drinking again. I expected a totally different reaction. I thought I had set him free and that we could stop moving from place to place—stop running from an imaginary state sponsored goon squad. But… My girlfriend… Maritza… She's been trying to get me to talk about it, but I have nothing to say to her. We were supposed to get married. But, she wants to have kids. How can I bring a kid into this world?

NINETY-TWO: Your girlfriend is right about having children. They give you small pieces of your family back. Like my son has the very same birthmark that-

REY: That's bullshit! My family's DNA ends with me! Cash, are we going to play or what? *(Rey walks quickly to John's table and sits.)*

CASH: Let's get it on!

JOHN: Don't forget about your kid's bike, Cash, and my hand! My hand! My fucking hand! No pressure. Breathe deep.

CHESS GAME #10
"Deflection"
[White-Rey] [Black-Cash]

1.e2-e4 e7-e5 2.Ng1-f3 Nb1-c6 3. Bf1-c4 Ng8-f6 4.d2-d4 exd4 5.O-O Bf8-c5 6.e4-e5 d7-d5 7.e5xf6 d5xc4 8.Rf1-e1+ Bc8-e6 9.Nf3-g5 Qd8-d5 10.Nb1-c3 Qd5-f5 11.Nc-e4 O-O-O 12.g2-g4 Qf5-e5 13.Ng5xe6 f7xe6 4.f6xg7 Rh8-g8 15.Bc1-h6 Bc5-d6. 16.f2-f4 Qe5-a5 17.Qd1-f3 Qa5-d5 18.g4-g5 Bd6-c5 19.Kg1-g2 Bc5-e7 20.Ne4-f6 Be7xf6 21.Qf3xd5 Rd8xd5 22.g5xf6 Rd5-f5 23.Re1xe6 Nc6-d8 24.Ra1-e1 Nd8xe6 25.Re1xe6 d4-d3 26.c2xd3 c4xd3 27.Kg2-f2 d3-d2 28.Kf2-e2 Rg8-d8 29.Ke2-d1 Rf5-c5 30.Re6-d6

Cash starts the clock. They make a flurry of moves.

JOHN: They playing Gambit?

NINETY-TWO: Yeah, the Scotch Gambit! Max Lange Attack. They're going for each other's throats!

Move played:

Rey [W] - 17. g2-g4

JOHN: Holy shit, look at that move. G4!

REY: You can't take it. Right Cash?

CASH: I lose my Bishop if I do.

REY: It's going to get bloody up in here.

JOHN: I ain't worried. God won't let nothing bad happen to me. I don't understand anything. Who winning?

NINETY-TWO: It looks like Rey has a huge advantage. Rey is going to have a protected passed Pawn in the seventh rank after he trades queens.

Move played:
Rey [W] - 20. Qf3-xd5

NINETY-TWO: Which he just did. Rey has a winning endgame.

JOHN: Fuck Cash!

REY: How does it feel to be left with nothing?

CASH: It's only money!

REY: I think it's more than that. Your kid's bike. How are you going to deal with the disappointment on his face?

CASH: It's a long way from this position to victory, my friend. I just have to stop your Pawns from advancing.

REY: Grandmaster, Aron Nimzovitch, said Pawns lust to expand.

CASH: He also said that the passed Pawn was a criminal and should be kept under lock and key.

> Move played:
> Cash [B] - 21. Rd5-f5

CASH: Rook to f5 locks them up. Phase one has been accomplished—the incarceration of your passed Pawn.

> *Rey's cell phone rings. He's startled.*

NINETY-TWO: Answer it!

REY: Ninety-Two, please, there's a lot at stake here.

NINETY-TWO: Yes, there is.

CASH: How are you going to defend your f6 Pawn? Rook d6 doesn't work. Doesn't it lose the exchange or the f6 Pawn after I play Knight d8? I'm just asking!

REY: I don't believe this shit!

CASH: I think he just recognized that now his position is crumbling like Humpty Dumpty.

> Moves played:
> Rey [W] - 22. Re1xe6
> Cash [B] - 22. Nc6-d8
> Rey [W] - 23. Ra1-e1

JOHN: Cash is going to win the exchange. Cash, you too good! Fucking genius!

> Move played:
> Cash [B] - 23. Nd8xe6

REY: (*To Ninety-Two.*) See what you did? You made me lose my concentration. I get it now. You're all working together. What's your cut, Ninety-Two? What's your cut?

CASH: Hey look, I have my own passed Pawn, and she's lusting to expand! Oh, how she's lusting! Phase two is now accomplished. How are you going to stop her from queening?

REY: This is fucking insane.

NINETY-TWO: How many times have you opened a bottle of pills to take your life? If I'm wrong, I'll leave you alone. Four? Five? Ten? Fifteen times? HOW MANY TIMES?

REY: (*Pause.*) I've lost count.

NINETY-TWO: I've been there myself. One day, I took a hot iron and I started burning off the numbers the Nazis had tattooed on my arm. My mother walked in on me before I had finished all of them, and in a thick German accent told me, "Staying alive is the biggest FUCK YOU, you can say to those bastards who seek to destroy you."

REY: Those numbers tattooed into your arm at least tell you that what happened to you wasn't a figment of your imagination. All I have left are my nightmares.

NINETY-TWO: Your nightmares must remain your nightmares. You can't carry them into your waking moments because you'll end up a broken shell of a man talking to yourself. It is how many survivors end up. I've seen it too many times.

Cash makes a move. Rey's phone rings.

NINETY-TWO: That's your girl, right? She's reaching out to you! Answer it.

The phone rings again.

NINETY-TWO: ANSWER IT!

REY: (*Rey shuts off the call.*) LEAVE ME ALONE! (*The phone rings again.*)

NINETY-TWO: Come on, kid. Answer the phone.

REY: (*Rey shuts off the phone.*) There, it's off! She won't bother me anymore. Now, will you leave me alone?

CASH: I guess you came up short in this vengeance thing.

REY: You don't understand how good it felt to pull the trigger. We have to make things even in this world. For every one they took, we take one of theirs. An eye for an eye. A life for a life.

CASH: I hear you. But, right now, it is time to surrender. And you can go home and do some reflecting. You don't have to run anymore. Just live life and play some chess. Come by the park, donate some of your money to us. Just stop the clock, and we can put this day behind us. I'll go buy my son his bike, and the world will be in harmony once again. I'm waiting.

REY: I'm not you. I don't quit.

CASH: Nevertheless, we're now entering phase three—your resignation.

REY: My experience tells me that a winning position can't go to a losing position in just one move without blunder being made. It just doesn't happen. There has to be a refutation to your idea. There has to be. I'll find it.

CASH: I don't want to add to the pressure you are already feeling, but you're running out of time. John, it looks like today is going to be a good day after all.

JOHN: I knew God won't let me down?

REY: (*He studies the board intensely. Laughs.*) Got it! So simple, but so hard to see. Do you see it, Ninety-Two?

CASH: You don't have anything.

REY: Look at it, Ninety-Two. Didn't you say your wife wanted you to play? Do it for her. Make the move for me. I know you see it. You beat Capablanca. Studied with Lasker. I know

153

you see it. A diversion tactic! Are you going to play the move for me, Ninety-Two?

NINETY-TWO: I don't care about your game.

REY: Do you see it now, Cash?

CASH: There's nothing there. I'm from Missouri, you must show me.

>Move played:
>Rey [W] - 30. Re6-d6

REY: (*Rey slams piece down.*) Rook d6! Let me give you a little time for you to take it in... Double exclam! (*Exclamation.*) It's like a shot right through the heart. At the same time, it's such a beautiful move it should be in a museum side by side with the Mona Lisa.

JOHN: So, he just give Rook for nothing. So what? Take it!

CASH: Will you be quiet and let me figure this move out?... Dag!

REY: So, you're beginning to see it now! It's a paradoxical move. If he takes it with the Rook, I'm a Rook down but, then I get to Queen with a check, and I'll stop him from queening. After I give up my Queen for one of his Rooks, I can Queen my other Pawn. Right, Cash?

CASH: (*Seeing the predicament he's in for the first time. He's losing.*) That's a good move.

REY: Good move? It's a great move! I think it's time for you to QUIT again, Cash!

JOHN: Cash, don't tell me you losing.

REY: You better start praying for a miracle, John. That's all you have left when all hope is gone.

JOHN: God damn it! I don't believe this shit. God, why you keep testing me? I read Bible. I pray every night. I help old ladies cross street. God, could you stop fucking with me? Thank you!

REY: The Chess Goddess, Caissa likes me much more than you.

CASH: Caissa is—and will always be my lady!

REY: After we exchange all the pieces, I'll be a piece up, and then it's just a mop-up operation capturing all your Pawns. So, you might as well resign and spare yourself the humiliation.

CASH: Many a slip between the cup and the lip, my friend.

REY: RESIGN! Lay the King on the board. You're dead! You are dead!

CASH: Maybe, I can find a way out of this. You did.

REY: But, I have revenge in my heart. You're just trying to beat me for a couple of dollars. Dollars don't top revenge. Quit quitter!

CASH: You came here trying to work out whatever issues you're trying to work out. We have issues ourselves, and we're not throwing them around as if they meant something. My kid wants a bike. You can break but so many promises before that light goes out of their eyes. There was a time that when I went to pick him up, he'd run and jumped into my arms. Now, I have to go to his room, and he barely looks up from his game station. My chances are beginning to run out. And yes, a lot of fucked up things have happened to all of us. But right now—I just need to get him that bike. So, do us all a favor and stop with the bellyaching.

NINETY-TWO: Cash, please, don't make things any worse.

CASH: Worse than what, Ninety-Two? Most people on this planet have been wounded. And those who haven't been are most likely responsible for carrying out the wounding. I'm on that precipice, too. I wish I could've stayed in school. I'd be a professor at some overpriced university right now if I did. But I had to leave. My advisor couldn't understand how I went from a pleasant Negro, to an "I'll throw you out that fucking window nigger?" I tried to explain to him that the campus police had harassed me from the first day I walked into the campus. He sat there looking incredulous. Like I was making the whole shit up. Like it was all in my head. He said he knew the head of security, and he knew him to be a *fine* man. And asked whether I had been showing the department's letter informing security I was attending the school. Imagine this shit. I needed a special pass to walk in the university I was attending so I wouldn't get harassed by those hired to protect us. Let that sit for a second. It's like, somehow, he'd forgotten I had been at the university for two years, and, the harassment hadn't slackened off. Everyone reaches the tipping point. And, that night, as I walked to my dorm from the community center, where I taught chess, I was confronted by our on-campus rent-a-cops once again. And I just didn't feel like showing my freedom papers. So, I didn't stop when they asked me for identification for the thousandth time. They blocked my path. I'm a smart man. I knew it wasn't going to end well. And right before I received the very first blow of many from their nightsticks, I told these rent-a-cops that one day when they grew up, they might become real cops and their mamas were going to be mighty proud of them. I don't know how many times they kicked me—hit me—spat on me. My back hasn't been the same since—a constant reminder! The dean kept trying to minimize the event. I told him to stop displaying his ignorance. That he hadn't lived a day inside my black skin—shit a day—an hour! A fucking minute! This was history what we were talking about! HISTORY! And it wasn't just the campus police. It was also the doctoral committee, which was comprised of only white professors, who were already hitting me on my head over and over again with a metaphorical nightstick. I told him that it was easier for me to survive a bunch of toothless rednecks than it was to survive the racist scrutiny of the doctoral committee. That for them, I was still three-fifths of a man and that my brain wasn't included in that three-fifths. That the mere fact that I was going to be the first Black Sociology student to receive a doctoral degree from that institution, a mere sixty years after Jackie Robinson had broken the color barrier in baseball, said it all. He swallowed hard, and in the best waspy manner he could muster, he said he thought I needed downtime. Downtime? So, now I was a petulant child? A boy? With that, I was summarily dismissed. So, I decided I needed to do something where success wasn't based on what others thought of you. Where your ability would speak for you—not some preconceived notion of the color of your skin. What better place than the chessboard? Everything is clear in chess. A weakness is a weakness, a strength a strength. You know where you stand all the time. Sorry to disappoint you, but I didn't quit. I don't even know how to spell the word. I went down fighting.

REY: Is that one of those sappy stories you tell to get pity when you're losing?

CASH: Nah, my brother! Chess has given me something to hold on to when things around me are falling apart.

REY: You know what countries should do, Ninety-Two? Every country should unleash its nuclear arsenal and blow up this fucking world once and for all. There's no hope! Blow up the whole fucking thing already. (*To Cash.*) RESIGN! I SAID RESIGN!

NINETY-TWO: Kid! Come on!

REY: (*To Ninety-Two.*) Will you stop trying to save me! I'm not your father. I'm not your sister! They have to pay for what they did to Bernie. They have to pay for what they did to my mother. They have to pay for my little brother! They have to pay for what they did to my village. They have to pay! They have to pay. THEY HAVE TO PAY!

> *Rey opens his briefcase pulling out a gun, pointing it at Cash and John. For a moment, no one dares to move.*

CASH: Hey, hey, put that gun away.

JOHN: What you doing?

REY: You hurt my family!

CASH: We didn't hurt your family. Come on, put that gun away.

REY: You got to pay.

NINETY-TWO: REY! HEY, REY!

> *Rey points the gun at Ninety-Two.*

JEROME: Be careful!

NINETY-TWO: I got nothing to worry about. I have my flower. It won't let anything happen to me. (*Takes out flower.*) REY! Hey REY! You don't want to hurt anybody here. These guys didn't hurt your family. Cash, move away. (*To Rey.*) You're getting things mixed up. Rey! REY, look at me!

REY: STAY AWAY!

NINETY-TWO: REY!

Rey points the gun at Ninety-Two.

JEROME: Easy now, Rey!

NINETY-TWO: Rey, do you know where I got this flower from? I got it at the concentration camp. It was growing next to a barbed wire fence, on a spot where I saw countless people die. As I was looking at it, a SS guard came over and stepped on it, crushing the life out of it. When the guard left, my father picked it up and put it in my pocket. The next day, there was another flower growing on that same spot. The day after that, the whole camp was full of these small wildflowers. They were reminding us that life still went on. The guards made us pull every single flower from the ground. The next day, hundreds of wildflowers danced in the wind on the other side of the fence. It was as if they were laughing at the murderers. My father whispered in my ear, "Those boots, that army, could never conquer the spirit of that little flower. And if they can't conquer a little, fragile flower, how could they conquer our spirit? They will never win!" Come on, Rey! Don't let those murderers win. Give me the gun, Rey.

REY: STAY AWAY! Please, stay away.

NINETY-TWO: I know what you're going through. Remember, we are part of the same club.

REY: I can't do this anymore…

Rey points the gun at his own head.

NINETY-TWO: I know. I know. Rey. REY.

REY: The nightmares are never going away…

NINETY-TWO: I know… I know.

REY: When they pulled my mother's remains from the ground, they were wrapped in her shredded dress. I recognized the dress because she had sewn a giant sunflower on it. I can't get that image out of my head. I can't sleep. I don't know if I can go on.

NINETY-TWO: You can and you will.

CASH: Why don't you two play a game?

NINETY-TWO: You know I don't play…

CASH: Just make a move, Ninety-Two.

NINETY-TWO: I can't…

CASH: Jerome, talk to him. Please, we need your help.

JEROME: (*Pause.*) You can do it, my friend.

Ninety-Two looks at Rey.

NINETY-TWO: Jerome. Don't ask me to do that. I made a promise.

JEROME: You've kept the promise all this time. It's been fulfilled. Now it's time to give it a rest. Your family will understand.

NINETY-TWO: You know I can't.

JEROME: Do it for the kid. He needs you. Like a fisherman— cast your line.

NINETY-TWO: ... okay... Okay... Let's play, Rey. E4.

> *They play without moving the chess pieces on the board.*

JEROME: He made the first move. Come on, Rey, make a move. He's coming out of retirement just for you.

REY: ...E6.

JEROME: Now it's your turn, my friend. Make a move.

NINETY-TWO: ...D4.

JEROME: Your turn, Rey!

REY: ...D5.

NINETY-TWO: Nd2.

REY: ...Nf6.

JEROME: Rey, why don't you put that gun away? Guns and chess don't mix. Isn't that right, Cash?

CASH: He's right, Rey. Give me the gun.

Cash starts walking towards Rey. Rey points the gun at him.

NINETY-TWO: Okay, okay. Rey, look at me.

Rey turns to Ninety-Two, who's holding the flower.

NINETY-TWO: I tell you what, Rey. I'll trade you my flower for that gun. My flower can protect you much better than that gun can. What do you say?

Ninety-Two slides the flower over. After a short moment, Rey grabs the flower and almost collapses, then looks at it closely.

REY: My mother loved flowers so much. I used to run into the woods to find her wildflowers. I'd make her a little bouquet, and she'd light up. I loved to see her happy.

Rey slides the gun over to Ninety-Two. Everyone relaxes a bit as Jerome puts a handkerchief over it, grabs it, and quickly puts it his cowhide satchel.

REY: She used to say that love came from a happy flower that lives inside of us. And all we had to do was water it and give it sunlight so it wouldn't wilt.

NINETY-TWO: And she was right. She was right.

REY: I don't know what to do.

NINETY-TWO: Call your girl...

REY: ... Maritza.

NINETY-TWO: Call Maritza. Call her.

REY: I don't think she'll...

NINETY-TWO: She will. She was calling you because she cares about you. And when you get home, you, Maritza, and Bernie should have a long talk.

REY: Do you really see your family in your kids?

NINETY-TWO: Yes! Yes! My father's smile is in my son. My daughter is the spitting image of my sister, Leah. My mother had this crooked pinky toe, and my grandson has the same crooked pinky toe. Go ahead, call her. You're going to need a kind face to look at when you wake up from your nightmares. It soothes the spirit. Believe me, I know.

> *Rey presses the button on the cell phone and walks away for privacy.*

REY: Maritza!... Don't hang up! Please, don't hang up!... I've been going a little crazy lately... You're right. A lot crazy! But, I want to work things out... I want to talk about everything... I love you so much... I needed to hear that... Okay, Okay... Tell Bernie I'm okay... Can I call you back in a few?... Have to take care of a few things here... Love you... Call you back in a minute.

> *Hangs up. Rey tucks his shirt and puts the jacket on.*

REY: (*To Cash.*) Draw?

CASH: I accept.

> *They shake hands.*

REY: (*To Cash and John.*) Let's call the match a draw.

CASH: That's cool with me.

REY: I'm going to return all the money you guys lost.

CASH: I appreciate your kind gesture, but we can't accept.

JOHN: Why not?

CASH: Because he won fair and square. We pay our debts around here.

REY: What if I loaned you the money? I know you both need it.

JOHN: Yeah, Cash, what if he loan money to us?

CASH: That I can agree to.

JOHN: Me, too. (*To Rey.*) *You very good man.*

REY: (*Rey hands them money.*) No hard feelings.

CASH: We don't take things personally in this park.

JOHN: Sometimes.

CASH: Stand corrected.

REY: Cash, I didn't throw every game. Not game five. And your 13th move—the Rook e5 sacrifice—that was a brilliant move! You're a great player.

CASH: So are you.

REY: Would you please give this to Stuart? (*Hands Cash money.*) And thank him for me.

CASH: Will do.

> *Rey goes to Ninety-Two.*

NINETY-TWO: We are survivors. It isn't a badge of honor, but a burden of circumstance. The trauma we've suffered has made us all a work in progress. (*Ninety-Two looks at everyone in the park.*) There are way too many bad days. But every now and then, you have a good day, and it makes you feel almost normal.

REY: (*To Ninety-Two.*) I shouldn't have brought up your family.

NINETY-TWO: No, no, I'm glad you did. You made me see I'm still trying to save them. I should let them rest. Listen, as long as the man upstairs gives me a furlough, I'll be around if you want to talk.

REY: Can I see your number?

> *Ninety-Two rolls up his sleeve sticking out his forearm. Rey traces the numbers with his finger.*

REY: Nine... Two. Ninety-two. What's your real name?

NINETY-TWO: Adam, Adam Kirschbaum.

REY: Thank you, Adam... I need to get going. (*He turns to go.*)

NINETY-TWO: Boychik!

> *Rey turns back to Ninety-Two/Adam, who hugs him.*

NINETY-TWO: You're going to be all right. Take care of that flower, and it will take care of you.

JEROME: Rey, after everything our people have gone through, we are still here. That says a lot about our spirit. Make sure you take care of it.

REY: Thanks, Jerome. We'll play next time.

Rey grabs his briefcase, takes out his phone, and begins to exit the park. Ninety-Two follows Rey to the exit. Waves at him.

REY: Maritza, I'm coming home...

Everyone watches Rey leave the park. They keep looking outside the park after he exits.

NINETY-TWO: People are stories. You see them walking down the street, but you never know what events have affected their lives.

CASH: It's scary. We don't know how many time bombs are out there ready to go off.

JEROME: We're all fish trying to avoid the fishing hooks. Some of us are luckier than others.

JOHN: Old Indian proverb. You don't know man until you steal his moccasins and sell them back to him.

Everyone breaks out into laughter.

JOHN: What you laughing at? Something like that, right Jeromes?

JEROME: Yeah, something like that. It's a Cherokee prayer. "Oh, Great Spirit, grant that I may never find fault with my neighbor until I have walked the trail of life in his moccasins."

JOHN: That's what I said.

Everyone except for Ninety-Two, who keeps staring out the park, returns to their normal behavior. Cash takes out the crossword puzzle. John takes out his racing forms from his Bible. Jerome sits at his table, goes to make a move, stops, gets his satchel, and begins to put the chess pieces in it, cleaning each one with a cloth before putting them inside.

CASH: (*To no one in particular.*) I need a player. No experience necessary.

NINETY-TWO: Cash, you're a mensch.

CASH: So are you, Ninety - Adam!

NINETY-TWO: You finish with that crossword?

CASH: Need one more word. Will to live... Got it! Conatus!

JOHN: Your anus?

CASH: Conatus. Thomas Hobbes describes it as man's will to survive. And that will to survive makes man strive towards the common good.

NINETY-TWO: You really believe that?

CASH: I don't know. I hope so.

NINETY-TWO: Blood has been spilled over every single patch of dirt on this planet. I'm sure that there's an ocean of blood as large as the Pacific Ocean at the earth's core. And yet, in all that darkness, our ability to be kind amazes me.

I wouldn't be here today if it wasn't for the kindness of others. For every act of cruelty, there are a million acts of kindness. Otherwise, humanity would've ceased a long time ago.

CASH: Nicely said. If I return to school to finish my thesis, I'm going to quote you.

NINETY-TWO: (*Smiles.*) Are you thinking of doing that?

CASH: What?

NINETY-TWO: Going back to school.

CASH: It's a thought.

JOHN: Cash if you go back to grad school I go back to middle school. Ah, fuck that. I hate school.

NINETY-TWO: Ah, feel that cool breeze?

JOHN: Virgins can rest now. And better—fish come to park now.

CASH: Amen to that.

> *Everyone basks in the cool breeze for a short moment. Ninety-Two walks to Jerome's table.*

JEROME: You did good, Adam. You did good.

NINETY-TWO: That kid is going to cry himself to sleep in his girlfriend's arms for God knows how long.

JEROME: He's lucky to have a shoulder to cry on. (*Jerome continues to put the chess pieces in his satchel.*)

NINETY-TWO: Are you really leaving?

JEROME: You know where to find me.

NINETY-TWO: Jerome, would you like to play a game?

JEROME: You don't have to do this, Adam.

NINETY-TWO: I want to.

JEROME: Are you sure?

NINETY-TWO: Yeah. I think I'm ready to play again.

JEROME: Okay! Today is a good day to play chess.

> *Ninety-Two sits. They set up the pieces to the starting position.*

CASH: Adam is going to play.

JOHN: Holy damn!

CASH: I have to see this!

> *Cash and John dash over to Jerome's table to.*

JEROME: Come get your medicine, young warrior!

Ninety-Two puts the sleeve to his nose, taking a deep breath, then, slowly stretches his arm out, grabs a Pawn, and places it on a square. Everyone cheers. A slow melodic tick of a clock is heard as the lights slowly fade to black to the good-natured banter of the chess men.

DRAW!!

CHESS NOTATION.

Diagram of the Chessboard.

	a	b	c	d	e	f	g	h
8	a8	b8	c8	d8	e8	f8	g8	h8
7	a7	b7	c7	d7	e7	f7	g7	h7
6	a6	b6	c6	d6	e6	f6	g6	h6
5	a5	b5	c5	d5	e5	f5	g5	h5
4	a4	b4	c4	d4	e4	f4	g4	h4
3	a3	b3	c3	d3	e3	f3	g3	h3
2	a2	b2	c2	d2	e2	f2	g2	h2
1	a1	b1	c1	d1	e1	f1	g1	h1
	a	b	c	d	e	f	g	h

Each of the 64 squares has a name!

The rows of squares on the chessboard are called "ranks" and the columns of squares are called 'files." The "ranks" are labeled from 1 to 8 and the files are labeled from a - h. These numbers and letters convey to us where pieces are on the chessboard.

The moves are written in two numbered vertical columns as follows.

	White	Black
1.	e2-e4	e7-e6
2.	d2-d4	d7-d5
3.	Nb1-c3	d5xe4
4.	Nc3-e4	Nb8-d7
5.	Ng1-f3	Ng8-f6
6.	Nf3-g5	Bf8-e7
7.	Ng5xf7	Ke8xf7
8.	Ne4-g5+	Kf7-g8
9.	Ng5xe6	Qd8-e8

The first column is for the White moves and the second column is for the Black moves. The symbol for the piece is first, then the square on which this piece is standing, then a hyphen (-), then the square to which this piece moves.

**In the notation, the letters [W] (refer to the White pieces) or [B] (refers to the Black pieces).

CHESS NOTATION

These are some symbols for the chess pieces, and other chess notations.

All the lower-case letters correspond to the

squares on the chessboard. If a Pawn is on one of the squares; for example, e2, only the square (e2) will be written in the notation signifying the Pawn is on that square.

Capital letters correspond to the major pieces on the board. For example; K=King Q=Queen R=Rook N=Knight B=Bishop x=Captures +=Check O-O=Castles King side O-O-O=Castles Queen side.

When "castling," you simultaneously move your King, and one of your Rooks. The King moves two squares towards a Rook, and that Rook moves to the square at the other side of the King.

If a major piece like the Queen who's on b2 captures another piece, let's supposed a Knight on b8, it will be notated as such: Qb2xb8.

(x) indicates a capture took place so: 7. Ng5xf7+ means the White's Knight on g5 captured a piece on f7.

+ Indicates the opponent's King is in check.

Chess moves that correspond to dialogue will be written in the stage directions.

KING WITHOUT A CASTLE and "The Theatre of Fantastic Realism"

Cándido Tirado wrote KING WITHOUT A CASTLE in the theatrical style of "The Theatre of Fantastic Realism," which was developed in Argentina. He studied this theatrical artform with Argentine playwright, director, and theoretician Guillermo Gentile (b.1942 - d.2011). In his early career, Gentile studied playwriting with the poet, playwright, director, filmmaker Pier Paolo Pasolini (b. 1922 – d.1975) at Cinecittà in Rome. One of the main principles that Gentile learned from Pasolini is that story structures should feature "limited characters in limited situations." This condition would force characters to their very limit, increase the stakes of the story, and render a raw and honest reality to the world created by the author. Gentile explored this structure in his writing, but he felt that something was missing which left him dissatisfied. (Gentile.) After completing his studies with Pasolini, he began his quest for this missing piece.

During the late 1960s back home in Argentina, Gentile, along with other theatre artists, experimented with theatrical structures and styles and discovered that it is the "irrational" that drives the human experience. The irrational would lead to "fantasies," which they translated into a theatrical language. This was the missing piece for Gentile. The "fantasy" would be the foundation for dramatic action. Gentile continued exploring this concept of the "fantasy"—how it deconstructed the Aristotelian notion of causality and how it could be the impetus for the dramatic action of a play. "The fantasy is the entry point into the story (where metaphors are created), and the irrational is used to explore the innermost desires and dreams of the characters" (Gentile). He codified this experiment into "The Theatre of Fantastic Realism." While conventional Aristotelian dramatic structure uses exposition to explain a past event and a character's present action, The Theatre of Fantastic Realism propels the characters into the future—to a state of becoming. As Gentile's work in The Theatre of Fantastic Realism evolved, he began to call his theory "Theatre for a New Mythology." He used both of these terms interchangeably. For this essay, I will refer to his theory as "The Theatre of Fantastic Realism."

Here is a classic example of The Theatre of Fantastic Realism that Gentile frequently referenced—let us explore "the Alcoholic." Psychology and Sociology provide social reasons for alcoholism: depression, crisis, poverty, or heredity. The Theatre of Fantastic Realism posits a person's rationale for drinking is rooted in fantasy. If, for example, a man recently lost his "love," one can safely say he drinks to console himself. As his depression over the lost lover increases, he drinks more. But does he drink because he's depressed? Does he drink to try to forget? No. Within the logic of The Theatre of Fantastic Realism, the man's fantasy is that the alcohol is the woman, so in turn he drinks "her." What is inside the bottle isn't alcohol; it is the woman. He drinks her to keep "her" inside of him, giving him a sense of wholeness. In this case, alcoholism isn't a vice; it is an instrument of completion.

I would like to take a moment to differentiate The Theatre of Fantastic Realism from its cousin "Magical Realism." Magical Realism is a literary genre in which surreal elements of dreams or magical events are integrated into a realistic narrative story. A more straightforward definition is "extraordinary events occurring in the ordinary world" – the surreal is the real. The supernatural realm blends with the natural, familiar world, as is found in Gabriel García Márquez' work of this style, <u>One Hundred Years of Solitude</u>, where, in the fictional town of Macondo, priests levitate, people suffer from an insomnia plague, and it rains flowers.

Referring back to the example of the alcoholic, whereas "The Theatre of Fantastic Realism edicts that the alcoholic man is drinking the woman, Magical Realism proposes that a man who drinks alcohol can grow wings and fly" (Tirado). Both genres depart from a perceived idea of logic and reason but manifest differently. Magical Realism uses poetry and images to describe supernatural events occurring in a mundane world. "Whereas the Theatre of Fantastic Realism uses the language of action. The fantasy is the driving force of the story. The fantasy activates the action" (Gentile).

Cándido Tirado met Guillermo Gentile in 1982, where Gentile attended a reading of Cándido's first play, *SOME PEOPLE HAVE ALL THE LUCK*. It was a fortuitous meeting, which later was cemented when they were both members of

María Irene Fornes Playwriting Workshop at INTAR Theatre. Fantastic Realism made sense to Cándido, and he embarked on a new chapter of his theatrical journey under the mentorship of Gentile, to delve into the world of The Theatre Fantastic Realism. "The progeny of this union is Cándido's play, *KING WITHOUT A CASTLE*" (Solarstein).

KING WITHOUT A CASTLE is the story of a woman, Isabel, who believes that she has given birth to her husband, Daniel. This is Isabel's fantasy, and is it the driving force of the play. In Isabel's "fantastic" reality, Daniel will be returning to her, manifesting through her son Danny's body, when he turns 25 years old, the same age that Daniel was when he died:

> **ISABEL:** …When I gave birth to Danny, I could feel Daniel's presence. He was there in the room. Danny started to glow. That glow was Daniel. Then the soothing light went into Danny… Daniel promised me he'd join me on Danny's 25th birthday… The age he was when he died, so that we could continue our lives together.

Danny believes that his father was a soldier who disappeared while fighting in a war, when he was born. That is the story that Isabel has told him to keep him living within her fantasy. The play begins six months before Danny's 25th birthday. Isabel is already preparing for Daniel's return – she serves Danny beer, encourages him to play the horses, and buys him a Navy uniform.

179

The fantasies are front and center. They are not denied nor rejected. As seen here at the top of the play, when Danny is getting ready for a chess tournament. Isabel encourages her son to go and defeat the enemy, but also mentions that the dead King (Daniel) will resurrect. She deals with a dual reality, acknowledging the present and the future at the same time, anticipating Daniel's return when she mentions the word 'resurrect':

> **ISABEL:** When you checkmate the opponent's King, the war is over. The dead King then lies on the chessboard. (*Pauses. Looks at Daniel's portrait.*) But he'll resurrect in time for the next game. These are the only weapons you need to defeat the enemy. Go and win the war, my King! (*Pause.*) How do you feel?
>
> *Danny stares at his father's portrait, filled with rage.*

Throughout their lives, Isabel has treated Danny like her husband. He has gone along with the fantasy, not knowing anything else, as he recounts this to his wife, Soledad:

> **DANNY:** We've been playing this game since I was a little boy. She'd dress me up in a Navy uniform, and I made believe I was her husband. I protected her from all the assholes that whistled at her in the street... An innocent game.

> **SOLEDAD:** You're not a little boy anymore.
> **DANNY:** It's still a game.

Even though Danny acknowledges Isabel's fantasy as a game, he is a non-entity in Isabel's eyes. He is holding a place for her husband, Daniel. This has had a destructive effect on Danny. He suffers from painful headaches and feels the ghost of his father is trying to kill him. His father is represented on stage by a shadow, which torments Danny more frequently as his birthday approaches:

> **DANNY:** Hey, shadow, where are you? Here shadow, shadow. Here shadow! (*He looks under the table.*) Are you under here? Why are you hiding from me? Are you scared? (*Unbeknownst to Danny, the shadow appears on the back wall.*) I said, come out! (*Danny turns around to see an enormous shadow.*) So, you showed up! I didn't think you would. I'm tired of you sneaking up on me. I want to get this over with right now. Why are you standing there? Why don't you choke me, now? Ah? Come on. Jump on me like last night. Do it!

The game of chess plays a crucial element in Tirado's play. The chessboard is the only space where Danny feels safe and protected, where he feels whole. He sees himself as the King, and the chess pieces are his family:

> **SOLEDAD:** ...Those wooden chess pieces are your family. You're a piece of

wood. You and your stupid games!
DANNY: They are not pieces of wood. They're the only friends I've ever had. These chess pieces fight for me. They don't try to change me. They just allow me to be who I am. And they don't try to commit suicide when they can't get their way. They just get ready for the next battle, not like you.

Danny's fantasy is to kill his father. By checkmating the opponent's King, he is metaphorically committing patricide. Given that his father continues to haunt him, Danny must *continue* playing chess so that he can keep killing his father. Chess is a game of life and death for Danny, which he must win. Now that he's about to turn 25, Daniel's shadow has appeared with the expectation of taking over Danny. Indeed, if Isabel's fantasy is that she has given birth to her husband and he will materialize when Danny turns 25, that transformation will ultimately lead to Danny's disappearance. Since the shadow has made his presence known, it is now incumbent on Danny to prepare for the ultimate battle.

In a story that is recounted in the play, Isabel approached Danny and tried to make love to him. It appears that she sexually desires her son, but in the fantastic reality of the play, she desires Daniel. Danny was confused by this action, and Isabel realized that she accelerated her desperate need for her husband's return. Since Danny wasn't 25 years old yet, the timing was wrong for the reunion with Daniel. This was the first time that their relationship became sexual; even though she had always treated Danny like her husband, there were never any sexual overtones before this moment. After that incident, Danny decided to bring a woman home to be his bride, to serve as a buffer from Isabel. He finds Soledad, on a bridge, on the verge of committing suicide. She is the only survivor of a car accident that killed her parents. She is as lonely and distraught as Danny. He makes a deal with her; if she doesn't jump, he will marry her. She agrees, and he brings her home. At the top of the play, Soledad returns home from spending time in a mental facility after another suicide attempt. She is an orphan and desperately craves to be part of a family. Since the death of her parents, she is focused on her and Danny creating their own family unit. She carries her parent's ashes in an urn and holds onto them for dear life. Throughout her time at the mental facility, she believes she has found the secret to a happy family in television commercials, where she saw consistently saw happy families:

> **SOLEDAD:** Wasn't that a happy commercial? Oh, no! The movie is coming back on. Movies are so depressing. People aren't happy in movies, but commercials! Everybody is happy in commercials! I especially love picnic commercials. The family gathers around a picnic table, full of smiles. Families never fight at picnics.

It is the collision of these three (3) fantasies—Isabel's fantasy of Daniel's return, Danny's fantasy to kill his father, and Soledad's fantasy of the perfect family—that provides the conflict and engine for the play.

A conventional analysis of the play might lead the audience/reader to believe that Isabel desires to commit incest, but that is not the case. Much of Western theatre looks for "reason" and "logic." Gentile frequently claimed that Freud destroyed theatre by promising an explanation, a 'logical reason' for why things happen. Why do people fall in love? How do people maintain faith? They are irrational experiences. Returning to his mentor Pasolini—a single mother raising a son, a son tormented by an absent father, and an orphan desiring a family, are limited characters in limited situations. By adding their respective fantasies to this dramatic structure, Tirado creates in *KING WITHOUT A CASTLE* a clear example of a play written for The Theatre of Fantastic Realism. There has been a tendency to analyze the play from a psychological lens—where Isabel is crazy, and she only wants to incest her son. But according to Tirado and the precepts of The Theatre of Fantastic Realism, Isabel isn't crazy—she has the fantasy that her husband is going to return to her through her son when he turns 25, and that, for her, is as real as the sun rising in the morning.

Tirado states that "We all live with fantasies, and that is what makes us human." People create fantasies whenever they want to fill a hole in their lives. This is a universal human trait. Danny, Isabel, and Soledad create fantasies in an effort to find their sense of "wholeness"—There is nothing more human than that.

Carmen Rivera
Playwright/Professor
February 7, 2021

NOTES:
Gentile, Guillermo. Interviews. A series conducted 3/92 – 10/92.
Solarstein, Sol. "Fantastic Realism Comes to New York." The National Alliance, pg. 12, March 15, 1985.
Tirado, Cándido. Interviews. A series conducted 6/92 – 10/92.

Cándido Tirado's **King Without a Castle** is a sophisticated and visceral drama that is the most provocative and successful play about gaming that I have ever encountered. Chess is the ultimate game, simple yet unendingly complex, and is as relevant today as it has ever been. Tirado's brilliant melding of the strategic and tactical mentality of the chess player with the fraught, interpersonal dynamics of a family mirrors how virtual gaming has been predictive of social and economic behavior and has forever changed how we think about and live in the world. In other words, the game has gotten real. This play is about "play" - how games are a limited arena for humans to understand and play out their most basic fears and hopes; like chess, the play in **King Without a Castle** is deadly serious and the stakes are as high as life itself. The drama in Tirado's play is terse and complex, and the writing is brilliant as the play unfolds like a match between masters of the game.

MICHAEL JOHN GARCES
DIRECTOR
January 27, 2021

KING WITHOUT A CASTLE

A PLAY

TIME

The past, present, and future taking place simultaneously.

PLACE

Anywhere people are ruled by the past, but are struggling to change the present for a better future.

CHARACTERS

DANNY: Twenty-five years old.

SOLEDAD: Twenty-five years old. Danny's wife.

ISABEL: Danny's mother. Fifty years old but looks and acts twenty-five. It can be played by an actress in her mid-thirties.

SETTING

Isabel's well-kept living room. The fragile furniture, which must be at least twenty-five years old, looks and feels as if its aging process has frozen. There's a flowery sofa and many lamps distributed around the room. A large portrait hangs on the wall of Daniel, Danny's father, sporting a thick mustache and wearing a Navy uniform. On both sides of the portrait, there are vases with roses on small shelves. A small cuckoo clock is mounted on the wall. A telephone sits on a small table next to the sofa. There's table with a wooden chess set, a chess book, and two chairs. A holster with a sword hangs from the table. There's a small bookcase with chess books. A box with flower print, bigger than a shoe box, sits on top of the bookcase. In addition to the front door, there are two other exits; one leads to the bedrooms and the other to the kitchen and bathroom. The audience can see inside the bathroom through a scrim. A large tub sits in the bathroom.

Castillo Theatre Production – Cast and Crew

Danny – Michael Camacho
Soledad – Amneris Rodriguez
Isabel – Nancy Groff

Director – Guillermo Gentile
Assistant Director – Gloria Zelaya
Lighting Design – Marsha Imhof
Costume Design – Jennifer Ruscoe
Production Stage Manager – Pat Sosnow
Technical Director – Wilton Duckworth

Puerto Rican Traveling Theater Production – Cast and Crew

Danny – Francisco Lorite
Soledad – Selenis Leyva / Marilyn Sanabria
Isabel – Anilu Pardo

Director – Michael John Garces
Set Design – Troy Hourie
Lighting Designer – Shawn K. Kaufman
Costume Designer – Mimi O'Donnell
Sound Designer – David Margolin Lawson
Production Stage Manager – Shelli Aderman
Technical Director Steven Katz
Translator (into Spanish) Manuel Martin

ACT 1

SCENE 1

> *The lights come up abruptly, whitewashing the stage. Danny, holding a sword, is standing on a chair, facing the upstage wall, staring at his shadow with contempt. Danny, excitedly, notices the room filling with shadows. With a thunderous bellow, Danny jumps off the chair and confronts the shadows. He delights in killing the swarm of shadows that revolve around him as he speaks.*

DANNY: KILL! KILL! KILL! Kill babies. Kill soft, tender babies. Kill smiling babies. Kill virgins. Kill soft breasted virgins. Kill long-legged virgins. Kill the Whites. Kill the Blacks. Kill the Chinese. Kill the Russians. Kill Hispanics, too. Kill everybody. Kill to kill. KILL—KILL—KILL!

> *A light goes up in the bathroom. We see Isabel's silhouette. She's sitting in a tub taking a bath.*

ISABEL: The neighbors are going to call the cuckoo house on you again.

DANNY: (*Danny opens the front door, screaming out.*) KILL THE NEIGHBORS! (*Slams door shut, jumps back on the chair, and scans the room for a shadow to kill.*)

ISABEL: Danny, will you bring me my towel? I left it on the sofa.

DANNY: Get it yourself.

ISABEL: I'm dripping wet, Danny. I don't want to leave puddles all over the house. Bring it to me, please!

DANNY: I'm busy!

ISABEL: Busy doing what?

DANNY: How can you ask me that? You know I'm preparing for my chess game today.

ISABEL: (*Sucks teeth.*) I bet all you're doing is admiring your shadow.

DANNY: I hate my shadow!

ISABEL: Your shadow will always be with you, so you better learn to get along with it. And it isn't going to go anywhere if you take a second to bring me my towel.

DANNY: Okay, but this is the last time. (*Danny snatches the towel lying next to a floral summer dress, sniffs it, savoring the scent. Awakens when-*)

ISABEL: (*Anxious.*) Hurry up! My skin is getting wrinkled!

DANNY: More wrinkled than it already is?

ISABEL: Very funny!

DANNY: I'm coming in.

ISABEL: About time!

> *Danny's silhouette is seen as he enters the bathroom. Isabel stands with her back to him. He throws the towel on her shoulder and hastily turns to leave.*

ISABEL: Where are you going? Dry my back.

DANNY: I told you. I'm getting ready for a game.

ISABEL: Dry my back!

DANNY: No... I'm...

ISABEL: (*Sad.*) You used to like drying me before. What's going on, Danny?

DANNY: Nothing...

ISABEL: So, dry me! (*Danny reluctantly takes the towel drying her with rough strokes.*) Easy. Easy. Don't rub so hard. It's bad for the skin. Just tap the skin gently with the towel.

> *As Danny taps her back gently with the towel, Isabel lets out little moans of pleasure. Danny is also be getting pleasure from drying her.*

ISABEL: That's it! That's it! Yeah... You have such wonderful hands!

> *She turns around. Danny glances at her shapely breasts. Abruptly, he drops the towel and runs out of the bathroom, jumping on the*

chair where he stares at his shadow once again. Isabel finishes drying herself, puts on her panties, slip, and a bra she leaves unhooked. Isabel enters the living room. The bathroom light goes off.

ISABEL: Danny, help me with my bra.

DANNY: Look at my shadow. It's the shadow of an assassin.

ISABEL: Help me with my bra.

DANNY: (*Moving away from her.*) I'm going to assassinate my opponent. But first I'm going to cut off his arms, then his legs, then I'm going to decapitate him. After that I'm going to -

ISABEL: Couldn't you just beat him?

DANNY: No! He must suffer a painful, agonizing death.

ISABEL: (*Isabel catches up with him.*) Hook it!

DANNY: Stay back! (*Danny approaches Isabel with the sword as if he's going to attack her. She laughs and backs away.*) My mind is a sword— double edge stainless steel— ready to bludgeon my enemy, and have his gushing blood flood the chessboard. His defeated chess pieces drown on his blood. (*He playfully jabs Isabel with the sword.*)

ISABEL: (*Laughing.*) Stop it! Every day you fill this house with killings.

DANNY: Because I'm great at it. I'm going to be the best chess player in the world. Decapitating heads all over the world!

ISABEL: You can't always be who you want to be. I always had this wonderful feeling you were going to be something more than a mere chess player.

DANNY: You say that because you don't know anything about chess.

ISABEL: I'm just telling you about a marvelous feeling I have. Call it a mother's intuition.

> *Danny hooks her bra. Isabel happily puts on her dress. Pauses. Becomes grave.*

ISABEL: Danny, we have to talk. It's very important... It's about you know who— Soledad!

> *Danny lets out a loud a battle cry as he looks over his shoulder to find an imaginary foe, which he swiftly and enjoyably kills with his sword. Not satisfied, he hunts for more shadows.*

DANNY: I don't want to talk about her.

ISABEL: She's coming back today, Danny. We have to talk before she gets here. Zip me up!

DANNY: (*Continues searching for shadows.*) Don't you understand? After I win today's game, I'll be an international chess grandmaster. Don't you know what that means? I'm going to be invited to international chess tournaments to play against the best players in the world. I don't want to talk about her. I need to concentrate.

ISABEL: We're going to talk now! Zip me!

DANNY: (*Pulls up zipper.*) Every time we talk before a game, I end up with my head handed to me. (*Runs to the chess table.*) Look, I'm setting a trap for my opponent. I'm sacrificing a Pawn in the opening. It's a poisoned Pawn. If the idiot grabs it, he'll be in the receiving end of my wrath.

ISABEL: We're going to talk whether you like it or not.

DANNY: I need peace to kill. Peace!

ISABEL: How can you talk about peace when you know the moment she steps through that door the fighting is going to start up all over again?

DANNY: I'm an assassin today. Don't depress me!

ISABEL: What about me, Danny? Do you ever think about me? From the moment she moved in, I felt like an uninvited guest in my own home.

DANNY: Do you want me to throw her out? Is that what you want?

ISABEL: Was I the one who found her on a bridge about to jump? No! Was I the one who promised her she'd be able to marry me if she didn't jump? No! That was you. You! You brought her here against my wishes. You forced her on me.

DANNY: Please, stop. PLEASE!

ISABEL: Danny, Danny! She's spent this whole month in a mental hospital after she tried to take her life—again!

DANNY: You won, Isabel, okay? I got a headache. Happy? You see what you did? I can't kill with a headache. I'm going to walk into the tournament like a man condemned to death walking to a guillotine.

> *Danny falls to his knees. Isabel relishes that she has weakened him. Isabel sits on one of the chairs at the chess table.*

ISABEL: Ah! Come here. Come, my brave warrior.

> *Danny crawls over to her. He sits on the floor between her legs.*

ISABEL: Your Queen will give you the weapons you need to become invincible. (*Shows him chess pieces one by one.*) This is a Pawn. The Pawn is the army of chess. Here's the Knight. It looks like the head of a horse. The Knight is the marines. The Bishop is the air force. The Rook is the Navy. The Queen is the nuclear power of chess. Don't misuse her. You must always protect the King. You must build him a castle made of Pawns. When you checkmate the opponent's King, the war is over. The dead King then lies on the chessboard. (*Pauses. Looks at Daniel's portrait.*) But he'll resurrect in time for the next game. These are the only weapons you need to defeat the enemy. Go and win the war, my King! (*Pause.*) How do you feel?

> *Danny stares at his father's portrait, filled with rage.*

DANNY: Ready to kill.

ISABEL: Good! See! You need me the same way your father needed me to psych him up.

DANNY: He didn't play chess.

ISABEL: I know, silly. Before he went to the horse racing tracks! When I saw him getting out of a bus with a frown, I knew he had picked the wrong horse. But when I saw him getting out of a taxi with a beautiful smile and a bouquet of roses, I knew he'd chosen the right horse. (*She waltzes around the room.*) We went dancing out on the town, and everywhere we went, we took a taxi, like royalty! (*She spins, stops. Happy again.*) I'll get you a beer!

DANNY: You know damn well I don't drink.

ISABEL: (*Angry.*) You're nothing like your father. You don't drink. You don't play the horses. And you never come home in a taxi!

> *Danny picks up a Knight.*

DANNY: I like horses. I like my Knights!

ISABEL: I'll get you a beer.

> *She exits. Danny makes an obscene gesture at father's portrait, then goes to the chessboard and studies the chessboard. Isabel enters with an envelope and a beer. She hands Danny the envelope.*

ISABEL: Happy birthday!

DANNY: Today isn't my birthday.

ISABEL: Nobody celebrates their birthday on the day they were born, silly!

DANNY: They should!

ISABEL: You are so old fashioned! We celebrated your father's birthday for months. That's how much he loved his birthday.

DANNY: Well, I don't.

ISABEL: You're so silly. Open-up your card. Open it!

> *Soledad enters carrying a small suitcase. Danny glances at her and quickly turns his gaze to the chessboard. Isabel looks at Soledad and starts massaging Danny's shoulders, then cautiously addresses Soledad.*

ISABEL: Soledad! We were just talking about you, dear. Danny. Danny. Look who's here.

Isn't it nice she's home? (*To Soledad.*) You don't look well, dear. You're so pale. Isn't she pale, Danny? Look at her face. For a second, I thought she was a ghost!

DANNY: Cut it out, Isabel!

ISABEL: I'm just trying to have a pleasant conversation with my beautiful daughter-in-law. Tell us, dear, did you meet any interesting people at the mental hospital?

SOLEDAD: Why don't you go and see for yourself?

ISABEL: Oh, no. Not me. Mental hospitals are for crazy people.

SOLEDAD: I'm not crazy—just mildly depressed!

ISABEL: Whatever you say, sweetie.

SOLEDAD: (*Looks around the room.*) Where are my parents?

ISABEL: I put them in the closet, dear. I'll get them.

> *Isabel directs an angry scowl at Danny as she exits. Soledad glares at Danny, who keeps his eyes fixed on the chessboard. Isabel enters quickly with a box. She puts on a happy face.*

ISABEL: Here they are! (*Hands the box to Soledad.*)

SOLEDAD: Why are my parents in a box?
(*Soledad takes out two urns from the box.*)

ISABEL: They were collecting too much dust out here, dear.

SOLEDAD: That's so thoughtful of you, Isabel.

ISABEL: How sad!

SOLEDAD: What's sad? What?

ISABEL: It breaks my heart, seeing your parents in separate urns. I wouldn't want to spend the rest of eternity separated from Daniel.

SOLEDAD: You're right. Why didn't I think about that? (*Soledad pours the ashes of one urn into the other.*) Now, they'll be together forever.

ISABEL: Ashes to Ashes. Well, I'm sure you two have a lot to catch up on. So, I'm going to go buy my lottery tickets. Soledad, it is so lovely to have you back. Danny, don't forget about our little talk.

> *Isabel exits. Soledad places the empty urn in the box, then puts the urn with the ashes on the bookcase. She then sits at the chess table opposite Danny. He doesn't acknowledge her.*

SOLEDAD: You know... (*Pause.*) Every night, at the hospital... I heard the sound of your chess pieces pounding against the table. (*Soledad pounds on the chess table three times with her fist.*) The sound got louder and louder!... I hated it!...

I'd open my eyes, hoping to find you there... But you never were! Why didn't you come to see me? (*Shouting.*) DANNY, ANSWER ME!

DANNY: DON'T SHOUT!

SOLEDAD: LISTEN TO ME, THEN!

DANNY: I'M LISTENING. I'M LISTENING!

SOLEDAD: OKAY!

DANNY: OKAY!

> *Silence. After a few beats, Danny returns to moving chess pieces. After calming down with deep breaths, Soledad tries a new approach.*

SOLEDAD: Are you angry at me?

DANNY: I'm a chess player.

SOLEDAD: (*Soledad playfully grabs a chess piece.*) Answer me.

DANNY: (*Danny snatches the piece out her hand.*) I did.

SOLEDAD: You didn't.

DANNY: As you know, chess players need to control their emotions. So, I don't get upset when you try killing yourself. Not anymore.

SOLEDAD: I'm glad you're not angry.

DANNY: Why should I be angry? I only had to drop out of a tournament I was winning. Hey, it's not the first time I've rushed you to the emergency room of a hospital. It's your life, not mine. (*Danny returns to making chess moves.*)

SOLEDAD: Since you're not angry, can we talk?

DANNY: Every time you get fucking depressed, you want to take your life. (*Pause.*) I'm not angry.

> *Soledad reaches out her hand. Danny looks at it. Then, hesitantly rests his hand on hers.*

SOLEDAD: I missed you so much... Why didn't you come see me, Danny? Ah? Isabel didn't let you, right? Am I right? Danny, you can't listen to her.

DANNY: (*Pulls hand away.*) I was preparing for the tournament I'm playing in right now. I had a lot of work to do. (*Makes a chess move on the board.*)

SOLEDAD: You care more about those wooden chess pieces than me. I talked about it with my psychiatrist.

DANNY: About what?

SOLEDAD: About your chess pieces always being at war in your head. Even when we make love. It isn't normal.

DANNY: What's wrong with it?

SOLEDAD: Nothing to chess freaks.

DANNY: I'm not a fucking freak!

SOLEDAD: You're always imagining you're playing against your father! That's freaky! (*Realizes she said something she shouldn't have said.*) I'm sorry, Danny. I shouldn't have said that.

DANNY: I told you to never repeat it.

> *He gets up from the table and sits on the sofa. Soledad follows him.*

SOLEDAD: Isabel isn't here.

DANNY: I don't care.

SOLEDAD: I'll never tell her. (*Pause.*) Are you happy, Danny?

> *Danny shrugs.*

SOLEDAD: You should be happy all the time. I know why you're not happy. We're not a normal family. There are millions of normal families everywhere. Millions! And they're happy. They live in houses with white picket fences. They have manicured lawns and landscaped backyards where they have picnics with their families on the weekends. Remember my dream, Danny? My parents and I standing in front of a two-story house with a white picket fence—holding hands—smiling! Remember? Remember?

Danny gets up, goes back to the chess table. Soledad follows him.

SOLEDAD: I can't live here anymore. And I know your mother doesn't want me here. Let's leave, Danny.

DANNY: We can't.

SOLEDAD: Why not?

DANNY: Ever since my father left, I've been the only person in her life. I can't leave her alone.

SOLEDAD: We're never leaving then. Is that what you're saying?

DANNY: No. We'll leave…

SOLEDAD: When Danny?

DANNY: I don't know.

SOLEDAD: What about your father? She's always saying he's coming back. Do you know where he is? Because if we can find him, we could bring him back to be with her. And we'll be free to leave.

DANNY: I don't know where he is.

SOLEDAD: I'm going to write to the Navy and ask about Daniel's whereabouts. Is that okay?

DANNY: I don't care.

SOLEDAD: Good! I'll find him, and you and I could finally start our lives together—alone! You know, I talked to my psychiatrist about Isabel. He said she needed treatment.

DANNY: (*Angry.*) She's as normal as you and me.

SOLEDAD: Danny, normal people, don't act like the wife of their son.

DANNY: (*Pause.*) That's just a game we play.

SOLEDAD: I hate that game.

DANNY: You hate chess, too.

SOLEDAD: It makes me feel sick.

DANNY: It's a game.

SOLEDAD: A sick game.

DANNY: You don't understand it. That's all.

SOLEDAD: Explain it to me then.

DANNY: There's nothing to explain. A game is a game is a game.

SOLEDAD: A sick game.

DANNY: Don't say that again.

SOLEDAD: It's the truth.

DANNY: We've been playing this game since I was a little boy. She'd dress me up in a Navy uniform, and I'd make-believe I was her husband. I protected her from all the assholes that whistled at her in the street—an innocent game.

SOLEDAD: You're not a little boy anymore.

DANNY: It's still a game.

SOLEDAD: Is it a game, or do you like playing with her? Is that it? You like acting like her husband. I want you to stop playing.

DANNY: Who will play with her?... I'm all she's got.

SOLEDAD: Danny, do you think it's normal that she gives you a beer every morning you don't even drink? Do you think it's normal that for the last six months she buys you a birthday card? Ah? What about that broken clock? She's been waiting for your father to return to fix it for twenty-five years. Is that normal?

DANNY: She thinks you're the one who's crazy.

SOLEDAD: I'm not crazy. Just mildly depressed!

DANNY: If trying to drown yourself in the bathtub was because of a mild depression, I hate to see what you'd do to yourself if you were really depressed.

SOLEDAD: What depresses me is to be a nobody in this house. When I was on the ledge of the bridge, looking down at my parents, waiting for me at the bottom of the river, welcoming me with opened arms, and just before I let go, you walked up, and without saying a word, you stepped on the ledge and stood right next to me. You had this panic in your eyes. Like they were screaming for help. Confused. I told you about my parents and you told me about yours. And you said you and I had to be together and if I jumped you'd jump, too. But if I didn't jump you'd married me. I didn't know you but I said yes because I was going to be somebody in someone's life. Then you brought me to live here, with your mother... But... Here, I'm as alone as I was in my miserable life and the orphanage before that. Your mother is always between us. When you're not playing chess, she takes possession of the rest of your free time. I can't live like that, Danny. I can't. I need you to understand that.

DANNY: You're right! You're right! (*Demonstrating it on the chessboard.*) Every Pawn wants to reach the other side of the board to promote into a Queen, but not every Pawn can become a Queen. First, the Pawn must be a survivor because death lurks in every light and dark square of the chessboard, waiting for its next victim. In our lives, death is everywhere, too. Life is a game of chess. You survive or you die. That's all there is, Soledad.

SOLEDAD: I'm tired of surviving. I've been surviving ever since my parents died in the car accident.

DANNY: I find it exciting you survived the car crash, and your parents didn't.

SOLEDAD: I was unlucky to survive. It would've been better if I had died with them.

DANNY: You don't understand. Our fathers tried to kill us, but they couldn't!

SOLEDAD: My father didn't try to kill me. It was an accident. He crashed his car into the river when a truck ran us off the road.

DANNY: Fathers are killers.

SOLEDAD: You want me to hate my father because you hate yours.

DANNY: He wanted to kill you.

SOLEDAD: He loved me!

DANNY: He's still calling you to the bottom of the river.

SOLEDAD: (*Cries.*) Not anymore. I'm never going to try to take my life again. I promise you, Danny. I'm never going to do it again.

They embrace. They sit on the sofa.

DANNY: We're survivors!

They kiss and get excited.

SOLEDAD: I love you.

DANNY: Oh, yeah?

SOLEDAD: Yeah...

DANNY: I love you.

SOLEDAD: Oh, yeah?

DANNY: Yeah...

SOLEDAD: (*She kisses him as she talks.*) I saw a wonderful commercial on TV. The first thing you see is a big house. Then the father puts on a long white butcher's jacket, kisses the wife and kids goodbye, and drives to work in his minivan. The last thing you see is all the butchers at the shop smiling in front of beautifully cut pieces of meat. And you know what's weird? The butcher shop in our neighborhood has a help wanted sign. A butcher makes good money. In no time, we'd be able to have our own house like the butcher in the commercial. You would look so handsome wearing a full-length white butcher coat.

DANNY: Me? A butcher? (*Laughs.*)

SOLEDAD: (*Laughs.*) Yes! You'd look very handsome.

DANNY: (*Kisses her.*) But I'm a chess player!

SOLEDAD: (*Kisses him.*) Butcher's live much better lives than chess players. Chess players don't live in big houses, and don't make TV commercials. Butchers do. I'm sorry to say, but there isn't a future in chess.

DANNY: (*Pulls away.*) I bust my ass searching for the truth in these sixty-four squares. I'll do it. I'll make it. You'll see. I'm the best. The best! I swear it to you. I'm going to be champion.

SOLEDAD: That's a dream! A dream, Danny! Live in reality!

> *Danny gets up from the sofa, getting a magazine from the bookcase, which he throws on her lap.*

DANNY: Read some reality. Out loud! Read it!

SOLEDAD: I'm sure you read it a hundred times already.

DANNY: I have, but I want to hear it again. It's good for my ego.

> *Soledad slaps the magazine to the floor. Danny picks it up. As he reads the article, he encircles Soledad, who keeps turning away from him.*

DANNY: Explosion on the chessboard! A good chess player knows when to sacrifice material. Danny The Assassin, as he's affectionately known in the chess circles, is one of the strongest young players in the country. His play is brilliant and dynamic. His positional understanding and sacrificial combinations in the following game remind us of former world champions Jose Raul Capablanca and Dr.

Alexander Alekhine. However, the Assassin's killing instinct and desire to win can only be compared to Bobby Fischer's. Danny said, "I like to annihilate my opponents. I go straight for their jugular. I love to see their heads roll on the chessboard." Despite "The Assassin's" youthful temperament, he has a bright future ahead of him.

SOLEDAD: Take that article to the bank to see how many houses you can buy with it!

DANNY: This chessboard is my house.

SOLEDAD: You're right. You're just a piece of wood like those wooden chess pieces. They are your family. You and your stupid games!

DANNY: They are not pieces of wood. These chess pieces fight for me. They don't try to change me. They just allow me to be who I am. And they don't try to commit suicide when they can't get their way. They just get ready for the next battle, not like you.

> *In a rage, Soledad slaps the chess pieces. Some of the chess pieces fall on the floor. Danny grabs her by the wrist.*

DANNY: Don't you ever do that again!

SOLEDAD: (*Stares defiantly into his eyes.*) You're hurting me!

> *Danny releases her, then rubs his head as a headache comes on. Soledad grabs her parents' urn and sits on the couch. Danny*

> *picks up his pieces, giving each one individual care. Isabel enters, perceives the mood in the room, then picks up a chess piece from the floor, giving it to Danny.*

ISABEL: Danny, here's your Queen! (*Danny snatches it from her hand. She pauses, looks at Soledad, then happily.*) It's lotto time! Danny, do you want a beer?

DANNY: NOOOOO!

> *Isabel flinches, then quickly exits to the kitchen. Danny and Soledad glance at each other, but their eyes never meet. Isabel re-enters with a beer and lottery tickets.*

ISABEL: Danny, can you please get my lucky box?

> *Danny directs a murderous scowl at her.*

ISABEL: Never mind, I'll get it myself.

> *She gets the box with the flower print from the bookcase, then sits. She places the lottery tickets inside the box.*

ISABEL: Soledad, you must get yourself a lucky box to keep your most valuable possessions. And don't let anyone open it because it will lose its charm. And I'm not a happy person when I lose my lucky charm. Right, Danny? (*Shakes box.*) Good spirits of all my friends, come, *come* and help me win. (*Isabel takes out the lottery tickets from the box, pauses, and stares at Danny. Accusatively.*) Every day you look more and more like your father. You confuse me! Daniel and I would buy a whole bunch of lottery tickets, put the whammy on them, and drink ourselves silly. I feel lucky today. I know I'm going to win!

DANNY: Nobody wins the lotto.

ISABEL: What are you talking about? The other day this nice woman won over ten million dollars! I'd be happy with just *one* million to give to your father. Then he wouldn't need to join another war to make a living.

DANNY: People win when the lotto makes a mistake.

ISABEL: Then, I hope I make a lucky mistake. Give me a lucky number, Soledad.

SOLEDAD: Thirteen!

ISABEL: I said, lucky. Bah, lucky seven!

DANNY: There's no luck in chess. The best-skill player always wins.

ISABEL: I don't know what you have against luck. You were lucky to be born! Give me a number.

DANNY: Zero!

ISABEL: You can't play zero, silly. Forget it. Twenty-five. (*Thinks about what she just said.*) Did you hear what came out of my mouth? Twenty-five! The age your father was when he...joined the war. You're going to be twenty-five in six months, too. It's such a wonderful age!

DANNY: I wasn't lucky to be born. I was born because I was the strongest sperm.

ISABEL: You were lucky a horse beat your father for the abortion money. A number, Soledad.

Soledad notices Danny's painful reaction.

SOLEDAD: Three!

DANNY: (*Hurt, striking back at Isabel.*) I wasn't lucky. I clearly remember the chess tournament we sperms had. The winner would get to fertilize your egg.

ISABEL: Leave pornography out of my lotto tickets.

Danny snatches lotto tickets from her. Isabel laughs.

ISABEL: Give me that!

Danny pretends to give her back the tickets then pulls them away.

DANNY: See, I made the finals with another sperm. His name was "Lucky the Sperm." He looked just like me, too. The only difference was that I was searching for the truth of the position of your fallopian tubes, while Lucky was waiting to get lucky like people who play lotto. It was a matter of life and death. And FUA! I won my first trophy—your egg, which I quickly fertilized!

ISABEL: You were a lucky sperm, and Lucky wasn't so lucky. That's all. Give me back my tickets.

> *Danny again acts as if he's going to give her the tickets but then pulls them away.*

ISABEL: Stop teasing me... You like teasing me... Your father loved teasing me, too. (*Flirting.*) Give them back.

DANNY: No!

ISABEL: He thinks he's so tough. Soledad, did he ever tell you the hamsters' story?

SOLEDAD: What hamsters?

DANNY: You better not tell her!

ISABEL: Oh, yes, I am. When Danny was four-years old, he had a pair of hamsters. Papa and Mamma hamsters, and they had babies. Four of them.

DANNY: Five!

ISABEL: Five. So, A few days after they were born, we heard this ear-piercing screeching. We looked in the cage, and four baby hamsters had disappeared. Yeah, Mama and Papa hamsters had gobbled them up, and the last one was dangling almost lifeless from their jaws. Danny became frantic. Right, Danny? He started yelling do something— do something! But what could I do? That's when Danny sticks his hand in the cage and tries to pull the baby hamster from his parents' jaws. Mama and Papa hamsters clawed at Danny, slashing into his hand, drawing blood. But Danny wouldn't let go of the baby hamster. Finally, he was able to yank the baby hamster away into safety. Danny's hand was in tatters, but all he cared about was the little whimpering hamster. He saved him. After I bandaged his hand, Danny pulled out Mamma and Papa hamsters from the cage, and drowned them. Sadly, baby hamster died a few days later. He couldn't survive without his parents. Danny sobbed for days. I tried to explain to him that sometimes parents eat their babies. But Danny was so grief-stricken he wouldn't listen to me. I didn't know what else to do. So, one day, I took Danny to a toy store to buy him something I hoped would make him stop crying. That's when he saw his first chess set. He was so mesmerized by it, he grabbed the chess set and ran to the cashier. Since that day, he and those chess pieces have been inseparable.

DANNY: Now you're never getting your tickets back.

> *Isabel chases Danny around the living room, finally grabbing him, tickling him as he falls on the floor laughing. She sits on top of him and snatches the tickets from him.*

ISABEL: Give me a number.

DANNY: I don't play to lose.

ISABEL: (*Tickles him.*) Give me a number, or I'll disinherit you when I win.

DANNY: Okay, okay! Fifty. Your age!

ISABEL: My age? Hah! (*Pause.*) Fifty? Ah, you're a joker just like your father. Do I really look fifty? I don't look a day over twenty-five. That was my favorite year. Daniel and I were so happy. I truly believe people remain the age they were when they last saw each other. (*Walks over to Daniel's portrait and points to it adoringly.*) Look at that photo. That's the last one Daniel took before he went off to war. He was twenty-five and hasn't aged a second, and neither have I. We will both be twenty-five until the next time we meet, then the clock will start ticking once again. Soledad, do you think I look fifty?

SOLEDAD: ...No.

ISABEL: See? By the way, Soledad, last night, the maître d' thought Danny and I were a couple. Can you believe it? He even sent violin players to our candlelit table. It was so romantic! A night for lovers! (*Pause.*) Give me a number, Soledad.

SOLEDAD: I'm having a baby!

ISABEL: A baby?

SOLEDAD: Yes, a baby as in pregnant.

ISABEL: I know what a baby is.

SOLEDAD: I'm not going to be an orphan anymore.

ISABEL: Danny, don't you have anything to say?

DANNY: I'm thinking! I'm thinking!

ISABEL: Don't scream at me.

DANNY: Let me think then!

ISABEL: There's only one thing to do here.

DANNY: This is between Soledad and me.

ISABEL: And me! Who protects you from the shadows in the middle of the night? Me, that's who! Last night he fell asleep with his head resting on my breasts because it's the only thing that relieves his headaches. So, don't say I don't have anything to do with this decision.

SOLEDAD: I agree with Isabel. She should have a say.

DANNY: Are you sure about that?

ISABEL: Yes! This is a baby, not chess!

SOLEDAD: I agree with you, Isabel!

ISABEL: Stop agreeing with me.

SOLEDAD: I don't want to fight anymore. I want a loving and peaceful home for our baby.

We have to become a normal family. It's time to start loving one another like a normal family.

ISABEL: I don't love you.

SOLEDAD: I know. I don't love you either, but I'm going to start loving you right now.

ISABEL: I don't want your love.

SOLEDAD: I'll love you anyway.

ISABEL: If you love me, open that door, walk out, and never come back.

SOLEDAD: (*Soledad ignores her.*) Come on, everybody, let's start loving one another. Let's play a love game. Come on, Danny, let's play! (*She pulls on Danny.*) Look at me. I love you. Say it! Don't be shy. Don't keep it in. Say it! Say it with me. I love you. Come on, Danny. You'll feel better. Everybody at the psychiatric unit felt better after playing. Okay, watch Isabel and me play. Turn around, Isabel. We can't play if you don't face me and look into my eyes. I love you, Isabel. I love you. Face me, Isabel! Your grandchild loves you, too. We love you!

> *Isabel faces Soledad. They both smile.*
> *Soledad is overjoyed.*

SOLEDAD: I love you.

ISABEL: Get rid of it!

> *Soledad looks at Danny, then back at Isabel.*
> *Crestfallen.*

SOLEDAD: I hate you! (*Embraces Danny.*) Danny, she doesn't know how to play.

Danny moves away from Soledad.

SOLEDAD: Is that what you want?

ISABEL: We can't have a baby right now!

SOLEDAD: I'm having the baby, not you. Danny!

Danny puts his chess pieces inside a cloth bag.

SOLEDAD: Danny, answer me. Is this what you want?

DANNY: I don't know! I don't know!

ISABEL: Be honest.

DANNY: I got a game. I have to go!

ISABEL: You can't leave until you make a decision.

DANNY: I've told you both never to talk to me before a game. I have to kill.

SOLEDAD: Danny!

ISABEL: Danny!

DANNY: Danny. Danny!

SOLEDAD: Danny, what I'm carrying here isn't a game. You're a father now!

ISABEL: Danny, she can't even handle when you go to play in a tournament for the weekend. How is she going to handle a baby? You are going to end having to take care of the baby all by yourself. How can you become champion of the world taking care of a baby?

SOLEDAD: No more games, Danny.

DANNY: I have to kill!

SOLEDAD: No more talk of killing. The killing is over. It's time for happiness! Happiness is possible. In the hospital, I saw thousands of happy families.

ISABEL: Thousands? In the hospital?

SOLEDAD: Yes! On television. There's so much love on television. The reason we don't know about it is because we don't have a TV.

ISABEL: They kill soldiers on television.

SOLEDAD: You're wrong, Isabel. I watched TV all day and night, and I never saw a war casualty. I don't think there's a war anywhere. Peace has broken out all over the world.

ISABEL: Daniel said there's no such thing as peace. Peacetime is when countries prepare for war. If real peace had broken out, he would've been home by now.

SOLEDAD: Isabel, I swear, all I saw were happy families. And not once did they fight. And do you know why they're happy? Because they're normal! It's so great to be normal. Normal people have routines. Everyone has a role. We have so much to learn from them. For example, Isabel, you can learn to be a normal grandmother. And Danny can learn to be a normal father. Danny, don't you want to be a loving father who drives a minivan? The baby and I will wait for you on the porch when you return home from work, and we'll greet you with a kiss. Then, I'll serve you your dinner. You wouldn't have to do anything around the house, but eat – maybe put oil in the car, or mow the lawn. And I'll serve you a glass of freshly squeezed lemonade to cool you off. On the weekends, we'll invite Isabel over to have a picnic on our patio with my parents. That's what normal families do.

DANNY: (*Danny hugs Soledad.*) We can't have a baby, Soledad. Not now.

Long silence.

DANNY: I got a game.

SOLEDAD: How can you ask me to get rid of my baby when my whole family is dead? I don't have anybody in this whole world! I don't want to be without a family anymore!

DANNY: I've got to kill.

ISABEL: It's the right decision. You go to war now. Don't forget your chess pieces.

Danny grabs the bag with the chess pieces.

SOLEDAD: Just like your father.

ISABEL: (*Proud.*) Yes! Just like his father!

DANNY: (*In a rage.*) I'm not. I'm not like my father. I'm ME! (*Doubtful.*)... me.

Danny exits. Soledad runs to door screaming out.

SOLEDAD: If you don't want our baby, you don't want me. You bastard! Go play your stupid games!

ISABEL: Soledad, I know how you feel. I felt the same way when Daniel told me to get rid of Danny. I didn't have a soul in this world. I felt so alone. Like you. Soledad, I don't have anything against you. I want you to believe that.

Soledad exits to the bathroom. We see her three-dimensional figure crying. Isabel talks to Daniel's portrait.

ISABEL: See the things I must put up with because you want to play war?

The lights fade to black.

END OF ACT 1 / SCENE 1

ACT 1

SCENE 2

> *The sound of water filling the bathtub is heard. Lights come up in the bathroom. We see Soledad putting her hand in the water. The urn is on the floor next to her. She starts to take off her robe. Danny enters with his right hand clenched in a fist. He crashes into the wall and leans on the wall. Danny's in another world and is having tough time breathing. Soledad closes her robe and enters the living room.*

SOLEDAD: Hi, Danny... Where have you been? It's past midnight.

DANNY: Looking for my head. I don't know where I left it. I've been looking for it everywhere. But it's dark and I can't see. Then I thought I left it here. Have you seen it?

SOLEDAD: No, I haven't. *(Soledad grabs his hand, leading him to the sofa.)*

DANNY: I need to find it.

SOLEDAD: You're having trouble breathing.

DANNY: *(He lays his head on her lap.)* You know, it's really hard to breathe when you don't have a head. And I don't understand how I have a headache when I don't have a head. I just don't understand it... Taking a bath?

SOLEDAD: Yes. The baby and I will be joining my parents. They'll want us both. I'm glad you're here. I wanted to say goodbye. Danny, I want you to cremate our bodies, put us in the urn with my parents and throw our ashes in the river.

DANNY: Okay, if that's what you want.

SOLEDAD: We'll be happier being ashes.

DANNY: Wouldn't everyone, Soledad?

SOLEDAD: You must've lost your game today. I shouldn't have talked to you before a game. You always lose when I do that. Danny, before I go, could I ask you a question?

DANNY: Sure.

SOLEDAD: Could you please stop imagining that you're playing against your father? It isn't good for you.

DANNY: He didn't decapitate me this time.

SOLEDAD: No? Then, who was it?

DANNY: I could've chopped off my opponent's head with my Queen, with my Rook, my Bishop, and even my Pawn! I started picturing my father's face on my opponent before putting him out of his misery, but his face faded away until it disappeared completely. That never happened before. Then, I started looking for another face I hated. And from the King's shadow this tiny person materialized... Smiling! He asked me to let him live. I told him, I'm a chess player. I have to kill you. Then I picked up a piece to mate him... But my hand picked up the wrong piece. A Knight! He went like this. *(Makes obscene gesture with middle finger.)* Then he jumped on top of a Knight and rode away laughing! I yelled at him to stop laughing. That's when my opponent picked up his Queen and beheaded me.

SOLEDAD: Who was it, Danny?

DANNY: *(Terrified, he goes to touch her belly but pulls hand back.)* It was him. The little assassin that fertilized your egg!

SOLEDAD: Don't call my baby an assassin. He wouldn't make you lose. He loves you.

DANNY: He did! He did! You don't understand unborn babies. I was one.

SOLEDAD: I was one, too.

DANNY: An unborn baby never sleeps because he's always trying to figure out a way to cause the most trouble for his parents. I terrorized my father so much he joined the Navy. I know one thing, I'm not joining the Navy. I got to find my head! I got to find it!

SOLEDAD: *(Caresses him.)* Relax...Lay back...

> *Danny lays down on the sofa. She climbs on top of him. She kisses him, after a moment, he kisses her back. They get excited.*

SOLEDAD: Did you miss me while I was at the hospital?

DANNY: No.

SOLEDAD: (*Getting more excited.*) I hate when you don't miss me.

DANNY: (*Very excited.*) I didn't miss you at all.

> *Unable to hold back their excitement, they tear into each other, kissing and grabbing one another. Isabel enters, but they don't notice her. She watches them for a moment. Isabel turns on the lights.*

ISABEL: Who's taking a bath at this hour in the night?

> *Danny stops abruptly. Soledad continues kissing Danny in a desperate attempt to get him away from Isabel's seeming spell. After a while she gives up, moving away from Danny's limp body.*

SOLEDAD: My baby and I are joining my parents.

ISABEL: How romantic! A death-bath! Give my best to the in-laws.

SOLEDAD: I will.

> *Isabel exits to the kitchen. Soledad lovingly eyes Danny.*

SOLEDAD: Bye, Danny.

DANNY: Bye.

ISABEL: (*Isabel enters with two beers.*) Before you go, Soledad, would you like a beer?

SOLEDAD: No, thank you. Beers drive cars into rivers. It's a beautiful night for a homecoming. My parents are going to be so surprised. Bye, Isabel.

ISABEL: Wait! Don't go, yet.

> *Isabel grabs a rose from her flower arrangement and places it on Soledad's hair.*

ISABEL: Death likes beautiful girls!

SOLEDAD: Thank you, Isabel. Bye!

ISABEL: Bye.

SOLEDAD: Bye, Danny.

DANNY: Bye.

> *Soledad kisses Isabel and Danny, and exits to the bathroom. We see Soledad's silhouette closing the faucet in the bathtub. She feels the water, then takes off her robe and climbs into the tub. Isabel sits next to Danny on the sofa.*

ISABEL: I think I'm going to miss her. What happened to your head?

DANNY: You noticed! I lost it!

ISABEL: I'll help you find it. Drink your beer!

> *Danny grabs the beer, stares at it for a moment, then slowly brings it to his mouth, taking a sip, then guzzling it.*

ISABEL: To Soledad!

DANNY: Can you do me a favor?

ISABEL: Anything my headless King.

DANNY: Could you pull the Knight out of my hand?

ISABEL: Sure. (*She removes the Knight from his clenched hand.*) Where is the rest of the family?

DANNY: I just remembered where my head is. My wooden family is burying it in the chessboard.

ISABEL: Don't worry about it. You can always buy another family.

> *Isabel walks over to Daniel's portrait. As she speaks Danny undresses, then enters the bathroom. Isabel doesn't realize it. Soledad surprised, stands and embraces Danny, who then climbs in the tub.*

ISABEL: Danny, you must listen to your father. He always said, no matter how many times you lose to a horse, the next day you must climb back on that bus and go back to the racetrack. Your father is so wise. (*Looks for Danny.*) Danny? Danny?

> *Sexual grunts are heard coming from the bathroom. She goes to the door.*

ISABEL: Danny. Is she with her parents, yet?

> *No answer, just sexual sounds. She goes to Daniel's portrait a bit embarrassed.*

ISABEL: I'm sorry Daniel. Young people are always drowning themselves! But don't worry, things will go back to normal when you come back home. (*Takes a sip of beer.*)

> *Unbeknownst to Isabel, a huge shadow appears next to the father's portrait and moves across the room as the lights fade to black.*

END OF ACT ONE

ACT 2

SCENE 1

> *The set is the same as in the first act, except for a television sitting at one end of the sofa on a small table. Soledad, nine months pregnant, sits on the sofa watching TV, holding her parents' urn. She talks to her belly.*

SOLEDAD: Wasn't that a happy commercial? Baby Danny, our lives will be just as happy as a television commercial. I promise you. Your father has a great job, and he'll provide for us the way fathers do in the commercials. We'll be the happiest family ever. Oh, no! The movie is coming back on. Movies are so depressing. People aren't happy in movies—but commercials—everybody is happy in commercials! My favorites are picnic commercials. The family gathers around a picnic table, full of smiles and delicious food. Families never fight at a picnic. Commercials are so short. They should last as long as movies! (*Turns off the TV*). When the commercials are back, I'll turn it on. Baby Danny, I want you to know that the most important thing in this whole wide world is family. Because a normal family creates a safe, stable, and loving environment where a husband and wife can support each other and where children can grow in a safe environment. A normal family always has a warm hug ready for anyone who needs it. And you only see that in commercials. They're so real. My psychiatrist is so smart. I didn't know how much happiness existed in commercials until he explained it to me. Oh yeah, before I forget, today is your father's birthday, and I want you to be extra good because Danny is going through a lot right now. And he hates his birthday, so let's try to make him as happy as possible. There's another thing I must talk to you about. You must come out. You're two weeks overdue. I understand why you don't want to be born. I can hear you crying when Isabel, Danny, and I are fighting. I wouldn't want to be born into a family like this either. But it could be worse. Remember when I told you that my parents drowned in a car accident? That wasn't the whole story. It was worse than that. Like a movie! My father had been drinking, and he used to get abusive when he drank. So, he's driving, and he begins to slap my mother around. I was sitting in the back seat, and I start hitting him to make him stop hitting her. He turns around, slapping me with the back of his hand. But he lost control of the car, and it swerved into the oncoming lane. We were about to head-on collision with a Log Carrier Truck when my father quickly steered the car away, avoiding the truck. But we still ended up plunging into the river. See? There are worse families you could be born into. (*Talks to the urn.*) Mommy, Daddy, now that Danny is buying us a house, we're going to have a picnic every Sunday in the backyard like we used to have when I was a little girl. Didn't I tell you that he was a hard-working man? He goes to work with the same drive he had when he played chess. And you are both coming to live with us, and you're going to have your very own room. And we're going to be a loving, happy normal, family! Even you Daddy. (*Turns the TV on.)* Yay! The commercials are back. Look at how happy that family is!

> *Danny enters wearing a short blood-stained butcher jacket. He's now sporting a light mustache—not as thick as his father's in the portrait. He throws a couple of letter envelopes on the bookcase, then glowers at his father's portrait.*

SOLEDAD: Hi, Daddy Danny. Come give Baby Danny and me a kiss.

> *He reluctantly kisses her on the cheek, then kisses her belly with trepidation.*

SOLEDAD: Don't be afraid of him. Kiss him again.

DANNY: Later. It takes time to get used to a baby.

SOLEDAD: I said, kiss him. Do you want him to feel unloved?

DANNY: Later, Soledad.

SOLEDAD: No, you come and kiss him right now. He'll be living with us very soon and if you treat him like this now, imagine how you're going to treat him when he's living with us. He's going to have a loving family like the ones on TV. There's a reason why he doesn't want to be born. Prove to him you really love him. So, come kiss him. Now!

DANNY: Okay... Okay.

Veiling the terror he feels, he kisses her belly.

SOLEDAD: (*Happy.*) Uh, look, he kissed you back.

DANNY: I think that was a kick.

SOLEDAD: You must be hungry.

DANNY: No!

SOLEDAD: Danny, you must eat. If you don't, you're going to get sick, especially now that you're working two shifts a day in that cold butcher shop. Besides I prepared you a birthday dinner.

DANNY: I said I'm not hungry.

SOLEDAD: Relax! Let me help you with your jacket.

DANNY: (*He runs behind the couch, getting away from her.*) I'll do it myself.

SOLEDAD: Let me help you.

DANNY: I can do it myself. I'm not crippled. (*Wiggles fingers.*) See?

SOLEDAD: I just want to be a good wife like the ones in commercials.

DANNY: You do everything for me, except go to the bathroom.

SOLEDAD: Because I love you! The man who comes home after working all day shouldn't have to move a finger.

DANNY: But I like moving my fingers!

SOLEDAD: (*Upset.*) Men on TV never complain when their wives do everything for them.

DANNY: Okay, Soledad. Take off my jacket.

SOLEDAD: (*She happily takes off his jacket, smelling it.*) You smell like a dead cow!

DANNY: Chickens! I butcher chickens, not cows.

SOLEDAD: If you keep working hard, one day you'll get promoted to butchering cows. A butcher has a promising future. How's your headache?

DANNY: (*Lies.*) It's gone.

SOLEDAD: It's hard to believe that a headache you've had for a whole year left just like that.

DANNY: Well, it has. (*Danny scans the living room, then looks in the kitchen, bathroom and bedroom.*) Where's Isabel?

SOLEDAD: She went to the butcher shop to take your measurements.

DANNY: I know that. Where is she now?

SOLEDAD: She hasn't come back.

DANNY: Shit!

SOLEDAD: The baby, Danny.

DANNY: Sorry.

SOLEDAD: What's the matter, Danny?

DANNY: The butcher shop is where I work, not where I get my measurements taken.

SOLEDAD: I warned her not to go to your place of work. She could've waited until you got home to take your measurements.

DANNY: Fucking measurements!

SOLEDAD: Watch your language!

DANNY: Sorry.

SOLEDAD: Relax, Danny. Take deep breaths. *(She pulls him by the hand to the chess table.)* Let me see your hands.

DANNY: They're clean.

SOLEDAD: Let me see them.

He shows her his hands.

SOLEDAD: Why are your hands swollen? You had another fight, didn't you?

DANNY: The fucking foreman! I should've killed him.

SOLEDAD: Why, Danny?

DANNY: No reason.

SOLEDAD: What happened?

DANNY: Nothing! He's a pig. So, I quit. But don't worry, Soledad, I'll get a better job.

SOLEDAD: Where are you going to find a better job? Did you know that I talked to a real estate agent today about a house? It's a perfect house for us. Three bedrooms, a garden, and two garages! When I told the agent my husband is a butcher, he said to come right over. We can't lose the house because you decided to have a fight with your foreman. Call the him right now and apologize.

DANNY: If I ever see his face again, I'll kill him.

SOLEDAD: Since you won't call him, I will. (*Picks up the telephone and dials.*)

DANNY: Don't call him.

SOLEDAD: Forgive him, Danny. You must make peace with him. You have to learn to talk things out—to express your feelings, and remember, it's about making peace!... Hello, may I please speak to the foreman, please? Danny, you need to set a good example for our baby... Oh, hi, this is Soledad. Soledad, Danny's wife... Oh, I'm fine. The baby will be arriving soon. I'll take him to the butcher shop to introduce him to you. I called because Danny wants to talk to you. (*Covers mouthpiece.*) Here, Danny! HERE!

DANNY: (*Danny reluctantly takes the phone. Speaks in a friendly manner.*) Hi, boss. Listen, could you please do me a favor? Could you take all the chickens in the shop and shove them up your ass? Thanks a lot. Say hello to the boys for me. (*Slams down the phone.*)

SOLEDAD: Have you forgotten about your family? I can't believe you did that in front of the baby. (*She shields the baby by putting her hands on her belly.*) I hope he didn't hear you.

Danny runs into the kitchen.

SOLEDAD: Where are you going? We haven't finished talking. Tomorrow, you're going to march back to the butcher shop and get your job back. Do you hear me? Don't worry, Baby, your father will have his job back by the time you decide to join us.

Danny returns, drinking a beer.

SOLEDAD: You promised me last night, you were going to stop drinking.

DANNY: I was drunk!

SOLEDAD: Danny, cars don't drive themselves into the river. Drunk people drive them.

DANNY: Don't worry, Soledad. We don't have a car. I don't even know how to drive.

SOLEDAD: Last night you were screaming in your sleep again. You shouldn't drink before going to sleep.

DANNY: I wasn't sleeping when I screamed.

SOLEDAD: So why did you scream?

DANNY: My shadow jumped off the wall and grabbed me by the neck. It was trying to choke me again. I couldn't breathe. That's all!

SOLEDAD: That's the first time it attacked you while you were awake.

DANNY: It's not the first time. For the last few weeks, my shadow has been jumping on me. It usually misses falling to the ground next to me, then it climbs back on the wall full of shame. But last night it succeeded. Luckily, I was awake. I'm afraid if it catches me sleeping, it'll kill me.

SOLEDAD: I talked to my psychiatrist about your shadow.

DANNY: My shadow is my problem.

SOLEDAD: The problem you're having with your shadow is my fault.

DANNY: Did your psychiatrist tell you that?

SOLEDAD: He said, you feel choked because I asked you to stop playing chess and get a job. He said I should've weaned you off chess first. Danny, I'm your shadow! I'm sorry. Please, forgive me.

DANNY: You're not my shadow, Soledad.

SOLEDAD: My psychiatrist said I was.

DANNY: He's wrong!

SOLEDAD: He knows everything. He can help you. He said that you must play chess again, but as a hobby.

DANNY: (*Kneels in front of Soledad.*) Choke me!

SOLEDAD: What?

DANNY: Choke me!

SOLEDAD: I don't want to choke you.

DANNY: (*Shouting.*) Do it!

SOLEDAD: I don't want to.

DANNY: Choke me!

SOLEDAD: No!

DANNY: Please... Choke me. Do it!

SOLEDAD: Okay, okay. But if it hurts, I'll...

DANNY: (*Shouting.*) DO IT!

SOLEDAD: (*Shouting.*) OKAY! (*She chokes him with all the strength she could muster.*)

DANNY: Harder!

SOLEDAD: Come on, Danny.

DANNY: Harder.

SOLEDAD: I don't want to hurt you.

DANNY: Harder, goddamn it! Harder!

SOLEDAD: Okay! (*She chokes him with all her strength she has left, gets tired, then stops.*)

DANNY: See? You can't be the shadow. My shadow doesn't get tired. His hands are like a vice, and once it has me by the neck, I can't escape it unless I turn on all the lights. Tonight, we're leaving all the lights on.

SOLEDAD: You must play chess again. And you can teach our baby to play. I'd love to see you two play together like a normal family.

DANNY: I don't even remember how the pieces move anymore. They refuse to fight for me. They sit on their squares, laughing at me, waiting to be captured. Even the butchers beat me. I never want to play again.

SOLEDAD: You lost your confidence. Come here! COME!

Danny kneels besides her.

SOLEDAD: Concentrate. Close your eyes. Imagine a beautiful chess set. You see the Pawn? (*He nods.*) The Pawn is the baby of the family. The Knight is the playful cousin. The Bishop is the wise uncle. The Rook is the grandfather. The Queen is the mother like me. And the King is the father like you. How do you feel?

DANNY: Sleepy!

SOLEDAD: You're not trying! Remember, Danny, the joy we used to feel after you decapitated your opponent's Kings? Then, we'd make love till dawn. We don't make love anymore.

DANNY: You're pregnant.

SOLEDAD: We don't make love because you stopped playing chess.

DANNY: Your psychiatrist doesn't know what he's talking about, Soledad.

SOLEDAD: Play chess. Here! (*She gives him a box.*)

DANNY: What is it?

SOLEDAD: Happy birthday!

> *Danny looks at the box as if he's looking at a poisonous snake.*

SOLEDAD: A hard-working man needs to eat. (*She exits to the kitchen.*)

> *Danny throws the box on the sofa and begins to search for his shadow.*

DANNY: (*Whispers.*) Hey, shadow, where are you? Here shadow, shadow. Here shadow! (*He looks under the table.*) Are you under here? Why are you hiding from me? Are you scared? (*Unbeknownst to Danny, an enormous Shadow appears on the back wall.*) I said, come out! (*Danny turns around to see the Shadow.*) So, you showed up! I didn't think you would. I'm tired of you sneaking up on me. I want to get this over with right now. Why are you standing there? Why don't you choke me, now? Ah? Come on. Jump on me like last night. Do it! Are you scared? (*He raises his fists.*) Come on, fight! (*He boxes with his Shadow until he's totally exhausted. He falls to his knees.*) Why are you doing this to me? Why don't you leave me alone? LEAVE ME ALONE! (*Pause.*) You're not a nice shadow. You're not very friendly. Say your last prayer, Mr. Shadow! (*He tries to choke the Shadow. He struggles with it for a few moments, then releases the it.*) I can't kill you because I'd be killing myself, but if I kill myself, I'd be killing you... Stalemate! I need to sleep. But I can't unless you promise not to choke me. I bet you thought you had me last night, right? You had me pinned to the floor. But you won't get me, mister. Because I'm a survivor! Ahggghh! (*Holds his head.*) The headache is getting worse. There's a war going on inside my head. The bright lights make the pain sharper like somebody is hammering a nail into my head, but I can't turn them off because the darkness gives you strength. You didn't know I knew that! Ahggghh! My head. Don't tell my Soledad about my headache... You look tired, too. Let's make a deal since we're stuck together. Let's be friends. Want a drink? (*Drinks beer.*) Feels good, ah? I never had a friend before. A friend to drink or talk to. Are you a father? I'm going to be a father. My baby is angry because I didn't want him at first. But he fought me! I don't want him to hate me. Soledad thinks it was Isabel who talked me into not wanting the baby. But she had nothing to do with it. I didn't want to bring a baby into this family. I don't want him to go through what I went through. If Soledad would've shown me that she would be willing to fight for us instead of trying to kill herself when things don't go right, maybe I would've accepted the baby from the start. I don't know why he wants to be born. I wish I was aborted. You're a good listener. I've never told anyone how I felt before. (*He takes another drink.*)

> *Soledad enters with a plate of food. She quickly places it on the table. She then turns to see Danny drinking with the Shadow.*

SOLEDAD: (*Alarmed.*) Danny, what are you doing?

DANNY: Getting to know my shadow. A toast! To our new friendship. See? It drinks with me. It does everything I do.

SOLEDAD: (*She takes the bottle from him.*) Stop doing that.

DANNY: Oh, oh. Mr. Shadow. This is my wife, Soledad. Soledad, this is Mr. Shadow.

SOLEDAD: Leave my husband alone. Do you hear me?

DANNY: He doesn't say much. The silent type.

SOLEDAD: Stop talking to it.

DANNY: But we made a deal. It's not going to choke me again.

SOLEDAD: You can't make deals with shadows. You can't trust them. They'll deceive you.

DANNY: (*Jumping around the room watching his Shadow jumping, too.*) They're very playful.

SOLEDAD: You don't understand. Shadows don't like being shadows. They hate being dragged around and being forced to spend their lives plastered against walls. They envy and would do anything to replace their owners. You can't befriend them. Come eat!

DANNY: (*The Shadow disappears for a moment.*) Where's my shadow? Where is it? Do you see it?

SOLEDAD: Didn't I tell you not to trust it?

DANNY: (*He looks for the Shadow, finally finding it on the upstage wall.*) Don't get too close. We don't know each other that well yet.

SOLEDAD: Danny, you must look at the light. When you look at the light, the shadows remain behind you where they belong.

DANNY: I've seen the light, Soledad. I'm going to play the horses. I could make more money playing the horses in one day than in a month being a butcher.

SOLEDAD: Gambling made your father miserable.

DANNY: But he was right about the horses. They're better than a job. My father was just unlucky. I'm beginning to appreciate luck. There's a butcher that has hit the numbers three times this month. There isn't a system to choose the winning numbers, but he keeps hitting them. I've come to the conclusion that he's lucky. I've been studying him. And I've discovered his secret. And that is, he really thinks he's going to win. That's what luck is about!

SOLEDAD: Don't be like your father. Be a good butcher, living in a lovely house with your happy family. We can make the basement into a chess room, where you can go after work and play.

DANNY: Butcher. Chess player. Gambler! What's the difference, Soledad? You always have to survive like a roach. Survival, Soledad. That's your shadow. My shadow! Everybody's curse. The only choice we got is to choose our own cursed shadow. I'd rather have the shadow of a horse than the shadow of a butcher.

SOLEDAD: That's your father talking. You're becoming more and more like him. You drink. You gamble. You fight. I don't know who you are anymore. I don't recognize you. And with that mustache, you're beginning to look like him, too. I rather you kill your father instead of becoming like him. Danny, think about your son. He's refusing to be born. And you can't blame him for the way you're acting. Take your chess set. (*Opens box revealing a chess set.*) Look! A new family.

DANNY: (*Danny retreats, and grabs the plate of food.*) I need a beer. (*Danny exits to the kitchen.*)

SOLEDAD: (*Turns on the TV.*) Uh, Danny look. They're showing commercials. Look, there's a man building a tree house for his son. Look, the wife is bringing him a glass of lemonade. Come! Come! They're so happy. Come look!

DANNY: (*From the kitchen.*) I'm tired of watching commercials!

> *Soledad sits at the chess table, her world falling apart. Soledad sees the mail on the bookcase, and sorts through the envelopes, then finds the one she was waiting for. She sits at the chess table, opening the envelope.*

SOLEDAD: Finally! I thought they'd never respond. (*Opens letter.*) Dear Danny blah blah blah. We regret to inform you we can't release the information requested without prove of kinship. Please, send us a copy of your birth certificate. Blah blah blah. It took the Navy six months to respond. For this? Danny!

DANNY: (*Off stage.*) What?

SOLEDAD: Where's your birth certificate?

DANNY: (*Off stage.*) I don't know. Where are the beers? There's only one left.

> *Soledad gets Isabel's Lucky Box from the bookcase taking it to the chess table and opening it. She searches through the papers, then opens an envelope. She's startled.*

SOLEDAD: I don't believe this! DANNY!

DANNY! I found your father.

DANNY: I don't care.

SOLEDAD: But Isabel knew the whole time that he's...

> *The jiggling of keys is heard. Soledad quickly puts back the lucky box on the bookcase leaving the certificate inadvertently on the table. Isabel enters excited, carrying a shopping bag. She's wearing tight white pants with a low-cut blouse top and high heel shoes. Soledad eyes the certificate and quickly slides it underneath the chessboard.*

ISABEL: I found it! I found it! (*She goes to the cuckoo clock. Disappointed.*) Shoot! He hasn't fixed it yet! (*She takes out a Navy uniform from the shopping bag.*) It's identical to the one Daniel is wearing in the picture. I got it from one of those little shops in the village. You know the type! The kind that sells anything invented by man. The sweet, little, old man recognized me after twenty-five years... I don't understand why he hasn't fixed the clock. One day Daniel and I were coming home in the wee hours of the morning, after dancing all night, hand in hand, heart in heart, when I noticed that cuckoo clock in the storefront window display. I immediately fell in love with it. And of course, Daniel being the gentleman that he is, bought it for me. But the little, friendly, old shopkeeper said it was broken. But like a knight on a white horse, rescuing a damsel in distress, Daniel said he would fix the poor broken clock... The little, friendly, man recognized me. He said I hadn't aged a second! Wait until I tell Daniel... What a sweet man!... Is Danny here?

SOLEDAD: Yeah...

ISABEL: Really? Where? I want to show him the uniform.

SOLEDAD: He had another fight!

ISABEL: Yes, I know! It was wonderful, Soledad. You should've seen it. Danny punched the foreman in the eye. The foreman grabbed a leg of lamb and threw it at Danny. But Daniel ducked, and it struck a butcher who was trying to stop the fight. The foreman then ran behind the ham counter. Daniel flew over the hams landing on top of him and they ended up inside the chicken freezer. Dead chickens were flying all over the place. Then everybody started to fight and to fling pork chops, steaks, and pigs' feet at each other. I hid behind the cash register. The next time I saw Daniel, he was strangling the foreman with a chain of pork sausages while two butchers were trying to pull him off. I took off my shoe to defend Daniel. But he started to curse and insult me like he always does when he gets into a fight. So, I put my shoe back on and walked out the butcher shop with my head held high. The last time I saw Daniel and the foreman, they were beating each other with a couple of turkey legs in the middle of the avenue.

SOLEDAD: You mean Danny.

ISABEL: Danny? (*Pause.*) Yes, of course. That's what I said.

SOLEDAD: Isabel, I'd like to talk to you about Daniel.

ISABEL: What about?

SOLEDAD: I wrote the Navy about his whereabouts and they wrote back--

> *Danny enters drinking a beer. He glares at Isabel.*

ISABEL: You were so wonderful. I've never seen you fight with such rage. But you forgot to fix my clock?

> *She gets the clock from the wall giving it to Danny. He grabs it, and throws it on the sofa. Isabel quickly gets the clock, cradling it like a baby.*

ISABEL: You're going to break it.

DANNY: It's already broken.

ISABEL: You told me you were going to fix it today.

DANNY: I'm not fixing anything!

ISABEL: You should keep your word. You used to keep your word.

DANNY: Where the fuck were you?

> *Moving towards her aggressively. Shows him the Navy uniform.*

ISABEL: Shopping! Do you like it?

DANNY: Get it out of my face.

ISABEL: What's the matter with you?

DANNY: Me? You!... You walk into the butcher shop like—like… like a slut. (*Imitates her by placing a hand on his hip and walking with an exaggerated swaying of the hips.*) May I see the foreman, please!

> *Isabel laughs.*

DANNY: What's so funny? (*He walks towards her aggressively. Isabel moves back, afraid.*)

DANNY: Who the hell do you think you are?

ISABEL: I just asked the foreman permission to take your measurements.

DANNY: You know my damn measurements!

ISABEL: I just wanted to make sure. That's all.

DANNY: Okay, so what did the measurements have to do with you smiling at him?

ISABEL: Did I smile?

DANNY: From ear to ear.

ISABEL: Did I? I don't remember. The foreman is very friendly.

DANNY: Bullshit! You liked the way he looked at you.

ISABEL: I didn't even notice.

DANNY: Don't lie. Everybody stopped working and started whistling. How could you dress like that to a butcher shop? Everyone there is an animal!

ISABEL: Oh, you're jealous.

SOLEDAD: He has nothing to be jealous of. Right, Danny?

Enraged, Danny, glares at Isabel.

ISABEL: Stay out of this, Soledad.

SOLEDAD: You went to the butcher shop to provoke a fight.

ISABEL: If men look at me, it isn't my fault.

DANNY: (*Danny throws the empty beer can against the wall.*) You're a cock teaser!

SOLEDAD: Danny, don't talk like that to your mother in front of the baby.

DANNY: Are you sleeping with the foreman? Answer me! ANSWER ME!

ISABEL: Why do you want to know?

DANNY: I want to know! Did you sleep with him? (*He takes Isabel's silence for a yes. Danny, menacingly walks towards Isabel.*) You're a goddamn bitch.

ISABEL: Don't scream at me! What did you want me to do? It's your fault. You brought her here! I had no one, while the two of you were up all-night whispering. Giggling. Moaning.

> *Danny gets closer to her. Scared, Isabel runs behind the sofa.*

ISABEL: What are you going to do? Hit me again?

> *Danny stops right in front of her. She cries. A heavy silence follows.*

DANNY: I've never hit you. (*To Soledad.*) I never hit her.

ISABEL: Every time you lose at the racetrack, you get drunk and hit me. Why do you blame me when you lose? Why? You're the one who bets on the wrong horses.

Danny looks at Daniel's portrait while Soledad looks at him. He tries to caress Isabel's hair, but she pulls away from him. Soledad grabs his hand. Danny looks at Isabel, then storms out of the apartment.

SOLEDAD: Isabel, are you, all right?

ISABEL: I'm fine, dear.

SOLEDAD: I need to talk to you.

ISABEL: Okay.

SOLEDAD: I want you to stop getting drunk with Danny.

ISABEL: We only drink beer.

SOLEDAD: Please, don't encourage him.

ISABEL: We're just having a little fun dear.

SOLEDAD: We must help him. If you sat with me to watch TV, he'd do it, too. And I'm sure Danny would go back to who he used to be.

ISABEL: There's nothing wrong with him, dear.

SOLEDAD: Nothing wrong? When we're in bed and he hears you turning on the water for a bath, it's like—like he gets hypnotized. By the time the tub is full, he's in a frenzy pacing back and forth. There's nothing I can do to keep him from going in the bathroom while you bathe.

ISABEL: That's been going on only for the last few weeks. Don't worry about it.

SOLEDAD: Why do you let him do it? You're his mother. It isn't normal to leer at your mother or to have your son leer at you.

ISABEL: He washes my back. What's wrong with that?

SOLEDAD: Mothers and sons don't act like that on TV. I need you and him to stop it!

ISABEL: Don't blame Danny. It's all my fault. But I didn't mean it to happen. It was Daniel. He knew how lonely I was. He always liked playing practical jokes on me.

SOLEDAD: What are you talking about?

ISABEL: One gloomy, lonely night, a light appeared making Danny glow after he had fallen asleep on the sofa. I knew that glow was Daniel because Daniel glowed at times, especially before making love. That glow was also present when I gave birth to Danny. I could feel Daniel's presence although he was far away. Baby Danny started to glow, then the soothing glow went into him. So, on that gloomy night, Daniel called me over. I climbed on the sofa with him. I started kissing him softly. Then the glow disappeared and Danny opened his eyes. He had this panic look. He was so confused. So was I. Could this have been a dream? Daniel lived in my dreams, too. But the next day Danny wouldn't look at me. Then I thought that he was also in my dream. I was so confused. Were both of them in my dream? That evening he brought you to live with us, and that's when I realized it hadn't been a dream. I need you to know something Soledad. I would never be intimate with my own son. It was Daniel's fault. He made me so mad. But now, Daniel is coming back for good. And he won't ever leave again. He promised me he'd join me on Danny's 25th birthday, and we would continue our lives together. Isn't that romantic? I love promises.

SOLEDAD: Daniel isn't coming back, Isabel.

ISABEL: He'll be here tonight. It would be nice if you went out—maybe to a movie. We haven't seen each other in a long time, and we have a lot of making up to do.

> *Soledad pulls out the death certificate from underneath the chessboard.*

SOLEDAD: Isabel. Daniel is dead! He was killed in the war. I'm sorry. I was looking for Danny's birth certificate instead, I found Daniel's death certificate. He died the same day Danny was born twenty-five years ago.

> *Soledad gives her the death certificate. Isabel puts it gently in the box.*

ISABEL: I know, dear.

SOLEDAD: Why do you always say he's coming back when you know he's dead?

ISABEL: How can I put it in a way you might be able to understand? There are dead people and there are *dead* people.

SOLEDAD: (*Confused.*) Tell me, Isabel, what's the difference between dead people and *dead* people?

ISABEL: Your parents are dead because you killed them here. (*Points to head.*) And here. (*Points to heart.*) You even kept their ashes to remind you they're dead. That's why you act like an orphan. I haven't killed Daniel. I've never dressed in black. You don't see his ashes around here.

SOLEDAD: He's still dead.

ISABEL: (*She smiles.*) Not to me. I'm sorry, Soledad, but I have to get the cake ready for the birthday party.

> *Isabel exits to the kitchen. Soledad picks up the Navy uniform, walks over to the portrait, staring at it. What does all this mean? Isabel re-enters with a cake and candles.*

ISABEL: Twenty-two, twenty-three, twenty-four. Shoot, I'm one short. Soledad, have you seen the box of birthday candles? Oh, never mind. I see it on the bookcase. (*Isabel takes a candle out of the box.*) Twenty-five!

SOLEDAD: Isabel, is Daniel the shadow? Isabel! Is Daniel the shadow that's trying to kill Danny? Answer me!

Danny enters carrying a six-pack of beer. He drinks from one.

DANNY: What's going on?

ISABEL: *(Isabel runs to the cake, lighting the candles.)* Surprise!

SOLEDAD: Danny, we need to talk. It's really important!

DANNY: Not now. Look, a cake! I love birthday cakes. Ah, look at the miniature racetrack. Look, little horses.

SOLEDAD: *(Desperate.)* Please Danny, come watch TV with me.

DANNY: Not now. We're celebrating my birthday.

SOLEDAD: *(Soledad is starting to meltdown.)* Don't say that. You always hated your birthday. Come Danny. You don't understand! Your mother... Come here! *(She pulls him to the sofa in front of the TV while Isabel sings Happy Birthday in a low voice.)* Look! That's my favorite commercial. The one with the man building the tree house. Look at how happy his family is. We can be that happy, too. Oh, no, it's over. Don't worry, I'm sure it's playing on another channel. There's the father again with that big beautiful smile! Danny, you too can have a smile like that. Wait a minute! That's not his wife. And those are not his kids. What's going? There must be some mistake. *(Changes channel.)* There he is again. But he's with another family. I don't understand it. What's going on? I'm calling my psychiatrist. (*Soledad dials the phone. Danny takes the phone from her.*)

DANNY: They're not a real family. They're actors.

SOLEDAD: Actors?... How can anyone act happy when they're not? (*Soledad is dumbfounded.*)

ISABEL: (*Isabel sings louder, Danny gets drawn to her, ending up by the cake.*) Happy birthday to you. Happy birthday to you. Happy birthday dear Daniel. Happy birthday to you. Close your eyes and make a wish, then blow out all the candles.

> *He blows out the candles. Isabel walks up to Danny, who's spellbound, and kisses him on the lips. Soledad watches in despair. Isabel then gets the clock giving it to him. Danny sits at the chess table and begins to fix the clock.*

SOLEDAD: (*Screams.*) NOOOOOOOOO! (*Soledad snatches the clock from Danny, raising it over her head to smash it.*)

SOLEDAD: Danny, NOOO!

ISABEL: Don't do it, Soledad!

> *Soledad gets a sharp abdominal pain and falls to her knees. She shrieks. Danny runs to her. Isabel grabs the clock from Soledad.*

DANNY: Soledad, are you okay?

SOLEDAD: The baby is upset. Let's leave, Danny. Let's leave. Now, Danny. I don't want to lose you.

DANNY: But my birthday cake...

SOLEDAD: Danny... The shadow... Danny... Your father... (*She screams.*) Danny...

DANNY: Shhhhhh! Don't talk.

ISABEL: Danny, take her to the hospital. Here! (*Hands him the Navy uniform.*) Happy birthday! Don't forget to bring me roses.

Lights quickly fade to black.

END OF ACT 2 / SCENE 1

ACT 2

SCENE 2

> *The lights rise halfway, Isabel is wearing a sexy dress. She turns off the faucet in the bathtub. She enters the living room. She's startled by Danny, who's leaning against the door in the darkness. She turns on a light. Danny is wearing a Navy uniform, and he's holding a bouquet of roses. He looks petrified. A thunderstorm approaching is heard in the distance.*

ISABEL: I didn't hear you come in.

DANNY: Ah?

ISABEL: Welcome home. Are those roses for me?

DANNY: ...Yeah. (*Gives her the roses.*)

ISABEL: (*Isabel places flowers on the sofa, then grabs two glasses of champagne, handing one to Danny.*) A toast. To us! That we may we never be apart again.

DANNY: (*They drink, emptying their glasses.*) I'm sorry I made you wait so long. I should've been here sooner. But there was a gigantic shadow, ten stories high, following me. When the shadow went over streetlights, they'd blow up. Then the moon had an eclipse and completely disappeared. The stars started to fall from the sky at first one by one, then by the millions, until the sky became a black sheet. The darkness chased me all the way home.

ISABEL: You're here now. That's what matters. The tub is filled with warm water for us. We can wash each other's wounds with rose petals. You used to like that. I'm so glad you're back. I've missed you so much. (*She refills his glass.*)

DANNY: Thank you. (*He guzzles it down. Isabel pours him another glass.*)

ISABEL: Come sit.

> *Danny sits next to her. She slowly runs her hand through his back, then through his chest. She gently caresses and kisses his head.*

DANNY: Be careful, that spot is sore.

ISABEL: (*Kisses his head again.*) Does it feel better?

DANNY: No.

ISABEL: I've waited for such a long time. I almost gave up. I need you to make love to me... My body needs to be kissed from head to toe. I want to disappear in your sweat. I want to be one with you—so connected that we won't know where you begin and I end. Take me inside your skin...

> *Danny kisses her, and she turns off the lamp by the sofa leaving the area dark, only their bodies can be deciphered in the darkness.*

Suddenly, Danny starts gasping for air, and falls to the floor.

ISABEL: What's the matter?

DANNY: I can't... Breathe...

ISABEL: Come back to me.

DANNY: (*Danny gasps for air.*) Turn on the light... Turn it on! Turn the light on!

ISABEL: You look afraid. Come here. I'll make you forget all your nightmares.

DANNY: The light...

She turns on the lamp by the sofa. Fixes herself up. Danny takes a breath.

ISABEL: What's the matter?

DANNY: The shadow found me. (*He turns the chess table lamp on.*)

ISABEL: (*She goes to him. Concerned.*) I'll protect you. Rest your head on my breasts. That's it. Close your eyes.

DANNY: I'm afraid I won't ever wake up!

ISABEL: Let's take a bath. That always relaxed you. (*She pulls him toward the bathroom.*) I'm so glad you're back, Daniel!

DANNY: Daniel?

ISABEL: (*Pulls on him, but he pulls away.*) What's the matter with you?

DANNY: I don't want to play anymore.

ISABEL: Play? What are you talking about?

DANNY: Yeah...The game we always played.

ISABEL: Game? What are you talking about? The horses?

DANNY: No!

ISABEL: Then what?

DANNY: Me! The game you played with me!

ISABEL: Look, let's go to bed. We'll discuss this in the morning. I've waited twenty-five years for you. How many women would do that for the man they love? You've ruined the beautiful night I had planned. Thank you very much!

DANNY: The game is over, Isabel. I'm not playing anymore.

ISABEL: What game?

DANNY: The game! The game! Me making believe I was your husband.

ISABEL: That's not a game. You are my husband.

DANNY: You're my mother.

ISABEL: I'm not your mother. I'm your wife.

DANNY: No. You're my mother.

ISABEL: Daniel, I don't know what happened to you in that war-

DANNY: I'm Danny...

ISABEL: You're Daniel.

DANNY: Danny. DANNY!

ISABEL: Look at the portrait. It's you.

> *Danny grabs the portrait from the wall, punching it. The portrait falls on the floor. Danny goes on his knees, ripping the portrait to pieces.*

ISABEL: Stop it! Stop it! Please, Daniel.

DANNY: (*Bellows, as he finishes ripping up the portrait.*) I'm Danny, DANNY!

ISABEL: (*Breaking down.*) NOOO! You are Daniel. You are! You're my husband. I gave birth to you. You are him!

> *She goes behind him, putting her arms around him. He breaks her hold. As her arms open, it looks as if she's giving birth to him. He stands behind the chess table, then turns to look at Isabel who's desperately trying to put the portrait back together.*

ISABEL: See, it's you. It's you!

The Shadow appears against the upstage wall.

DANNY: (*Danny gets a sharp pain in his head. He lies his head on the chess table and covers it with his arms.*) Arghhh! My head is splitting in two!

ISABEL: (*To Shadow.*) Daniel you're late! (*Isabel touches the Shadow's face.*) Why do you do these things to me? (*Points to Danny.*) Your son is right there. (*To Danny.*) Your father is here! There's nothing you can do. It's been going on forever. Fathers always take over their sons, and sons become their fathers. (*Isabel runs to the lamp turning it off.*)

DANNY: What are you doing? Turn it back on!

ISABEL: Don't fight it, Danny.

> *She turns off another lamp. As she runs to another Danny tackles her to the floor.*

DANNY: What about me? What about me?

> *The lights in the room begin to flicker. Danny gets another stabbing pain in his head. Isabel pushes him off of her and runs to the Shadow.*

ISABEL: (*To Danny.*) He's ready!

DANNY: (*Pulls sword from holster and stands behind the chess table.*) I'm ready, too. Make your move. Come on.

ISABEL: *(She runs to Danny and tries to get the sword from him. Danny pushes her off.)* Don't fight him, Danny! *(Isabel comes towards Danny again. He raises the sword to strike her.)*

DANNY: Get out of here. Go!

ISABEL: *(To Danny.)* You're not going to win! You're not! *(To Shadow.)* I'll wait for you in the bath. Hurry!

DANNY: I said go. GO!

> *Isabel grabs the roses and exits to the bathroom. We see her inside the bathroom taking off her robe, and sitting in the tub.*

DANNY: *(Sarcastic.)* Are you ready for me?

> *Whenever Danny goes to a lit area, it immediately goes dark, and it is accompanied by the booming sound of thunder followed by lightning. Chessboard squares are projected in lights on stage. He desperately searches for light in the room. Danny swings the sword wildly at the darkened area. He runs to another lit area, which immediately goes dark. He swings at the darkened area again. He begins to gasp for air. The area where he's standing goes dark. He runs to a lit area, which quickly goes dark again. He continues gasping for air, and swings the sword each time with less strength. Each area keeps going dark until there's only one square pool of light. He stands on it. He looks doomed as he gasps for air. Danny gathers his strength for one last strike. As he brings the sword*

over his head, the stage goes black. The living room is in total darkness. After a few moments, Danny appears standing beside the tub. He stares at Isabel.

ISABEL: Daniel, you're back. Be a sweetie and pass me a rose.

Danny gives her a rose. She smells it. He kneels beside the tub, kisses her on the lips. He gasps for air. Isabel caresses his face. The Shadow appears hovering over the bathtub.

ISABEL: Join me. Let's wash our wounds with rose petals. And we can start our lives again.

DANNY: (*Weakly.*) You are keeping him alive... You are keeping him alive.

Danny, gasping for air, pushes her head under the water. The lights flicker wildly. Raging sounds of wind and thunder is heard. Danny, Isabel, and the Shadow are fighting for their survival. After a few moments Isabel stops struggling. As Isabel's and the Shadow's lives slip away, the rose slowly disappears into the tub. Danny gasps for air. Then bright lights white washes the stage like a snapshot before going to black. The wind and thunder recede into the distance, dissipating. After a few moments, soft light illuminates Danny lying on the floor in a fetal position gasping for air. His breathing slowly normalizes. Soledad enters. She's having contractions. At first, she doesn't see Danny.

SOLEDAD: Danny?... Danny? (*She sees Danny on the floor, stirring.*) DANNY?

DANNY: Soledad... (*He sits up slowly.*)

SOLEDAD: Are you okay?

DANNY: Yeah...

SOLEDAD: (*Hugs him.*) I was so worried about you. Where's Isabel?

DANNY: She's with him. (*He points to the bathroom. Danny sits at the chess table.*)

> *Soledad slowly walks into the bathroom, stands in front of the tub, looks down at Isabel. She grabs a rose placing it in the tub with Isabel.*

SOLEDAD: Death likes beautiful girls! (*Soledad walks into livingroom and rejoins Danny.*)

DANNY: You're supposed to be in the hospital. Are you okay?

SOLEDAD: I'm having contractions but I want to be with you. I'm scared, Danny. I felt my father's presence hovering over the hospital bed.

DANNY: You have to get rid of your parents' ashes.

> *Danny looks at the urn. Soledad, follows his eyes, she retrieves the urn from the bookcase. She and Danny walk to the bathroom. Soledad places the urn inside the bathtub*

with Isabel. They walk out of the bathroom and Danny places his arm around Soledad's shoulders, and she places her arm around the back of his waist. They look out into the audience as a white light bathes them, casting their giant shadows against the wall.

SOLEDAD: We must look at the light...

DANNY: ...And leave our shadows behind.

Their giant shadows begin to shrink until they disappear. Soledad shrieks, holding her stomach.

SOLEDAD: Danny, my water broke.

Danny lays her on the floor. He gets a pillow from the sofa and puts it underneath her head. Danny kneels in front of Soledad's to deliver the baby.

DANNY: He's ready to be born.

The lights slowly fade to black. In the darkness, we hear the cry of a newborn baby.

CHECKMATE